NOT JUST A NIGHTWATCHMAN

NOT JUST A NIGHTWATCHMAN
My Innings in the BCCI

VINOD RAI

RUPA

First published by
Rupa Publications India Pvt. Ltd 2022
7/16, Ansari Road, Daryaganj
New Delhi 110002

Sales Centres:

Allahabad Bengaluru Chennai
Hyderabad Jaipur Kathmandu
Kolkata Mumbai

Copyright © Vinod Rai 2022

The views and opinions expressed in this book are the author's own and the facts are as reported by him which have been verified to the extent possible, and the publishers are not in any way liable for the same.

All rights reserved.
No part of this publication may be reproduced, transmitted, or stored in a retrieval system, in any form or by any means, electronic, mechanical, photocopying, recording or otherwise, without the prior permission of the publisher.

ISBN: 978-93-5520-362-5

First impression 2022

10 9 8 7 6 5 4 3 2 1

The moral right of the author has been asserted.

Printed at Parksons Graphics Pvt. Ltd, Mumbai

This book is sold subject to the condition that it shall not, by way of trade or otherwise, be lent, resold, hired out, or otherwise circulated, without the publisher's prior consent, in any form of binding or cover other than that in which it is published.

*Dedicated to the 11 athletes
who toil hard on the cricket pitch
to provide entertainment to the masses
around the globe and thus
generate plentiful resources for administrators
to rule the roost over those very athletes.*

CONTENTS

Introduction ix

1. Four Ghostbusters Pad Up 1
2. Taking Guard in the BCCI 23
3. Delivering on the Governance and Revenue Model 43
4. IPL: The Next Test 67
5. Making Cricket Win 88
6. Uncovering the Head Coach Saga 106
7. The Maidens Bowl Us Over 124
8. Off-the-Ground Misdemeanours 144
9. On the Front Foot 151
10. The Nightwatchman Retires 170

Epilogue 185

Apendix I: Resolutions Adopted by the GB of the BCCI (22 June 2018) 189
Appendix II: Ramachandra Guha's Letter of Resignation 197
Appendix III: Emails Sent by Office-Bearers of the BCCI on the Issue of Action to be Initiated against Hardik Pandya and K.L. Rahul 206

Index 215

INTRODUCTION

Cricket has been in existence since the early thirteenth century. In India, cricket has acquired cult status; it is not just a sport, but a religion. For many people, cricket is their first passion, their one true love. As a true connoisseur of cricket, I am no exception to this. However, the pressure of prioritizing education over any sport, leave alone cricket, got to me too. In the race to acquire minimal educational qualifications to become eligible for taking the Civil Services Examination and studying hard to qualify, I had to put my cricketing ambition on the back-burner. Nevertheless, I am a conformist—a true Indian who may subscribe to any religious belief by birth, but adopts the religion of cricket from the depth of his being! From Vijay Hazare and Vinoo Mankad to the present whiz-kids such as Washington Sundar, Mohammed Siraj, Ishan Kishan and Shafali Verma, I have followed them all.

My love for cricket aside, I had never contemplated getting into cricket administration. I had heard of legends such as N.K.P. Salve and Jagmohan Dalmiya managing the game as presidents of the Board of Control for Cricket in India (BCCI); thus, it was with some trepidation that I saw myself entering that portal, albeit by a quirk of fate, when I was appointed the head of the Committee of Administrators (CoA) by the Supreme Court in January 2017.

Compounding these fears were media reports of match-fixing, betting, conflict of interest and cricket administrators being forced to vacate their positions by the highest court in the land. The Court decided to step in to ensure that cricket administration did not become captive to a few who had come to believe that the BCCI was their personal fiefdom and they could administer it as per their whims and fancies and for their personal benefits. It was an earnest attempt by the Court to make sure that the game of cricket is administered and delivered to its fans in its purest form.

It was appalling to believe it would come to such a pass that the Court would have to remove a sports administrator. Any self-respecting person should gracefully step down if the highest court in the land was even remotely looking askance at his role. But thereby hangs a tale—a tale of limpets that clung on to the BCCI bandwagon for reasons that none would ever have imagined.

Incidentally, it was also a tale that shook the cricketing world in 2011, when two journalists, Sam Collins and Jarrod Kimber, started work on a film on the state of Test cricket. Their concern was whether Test cricket was facing the risk of dying. That was the time when the spot-fixing scandal had taken India by storm and the International Cricket Council (ICC) was engulfed in the controversy surrounding the Big Three model.[1] Speaking of their experience, Collins says: 'We very quickly realised that every single problem in the game comes back to short-term thinking by the people who run it.'[2] The two journalists went on to make a 100-minute documentary titled *Death of a Gentleman*. The film cuts through all the confusion and obfuscation in cricket administration with particular focus on the so-called Big Three in the ICC. *Live Mint* carried the following comment on the movie: 'Death of a Gentleman brings all the various stories of greed, wealth, power and corruption together in one 100-minute

---

[1] The Big Three are India, England and Australia—the major cricketing nations. More details in chapters to follow.
[2] Bull, Andy. 'Death of a Gentleman: Call It Optimistic, Call It Idealistic, but It's Right', *The Guardian*, 28 July 2015, https://bit.ly/3HBNkZc. Accessed on 2 September 2021.

film. Additionally, for those who like to see administrators look shifty and squirm, this has many such moments.'[3]

The documentary is an excellent depiction of the state of affairs in the administration of cricket and the driving force of its administrators. BCCI functionaries are invaluable dramatis personae in it and hence I recommend that everyone see it. There is much to be gained from its viewing.

Like the documentary, what I am about to narrate in this book about the goings-on inside the BCCI is equally spellbinding and worth a read.

I put some things in perspective for posterity as people must know the reasons for the Supreme Court having to spend several hours, in 47 sittings, from 2013 onwards to deal with a plethora of cases filed by state cricket associations. Why did one distinguished senior counsel of the Supreme Court, Gopal Subramanium, appointed the amicus curiae, spend about 50 hours trying to create an ideal administrative set-up in the organization? He quit, and yet another distinguished senior counsel, P.S. Narasimha, the second amicus curiae, spent over 150 hours merely listening to representatives of state associations who believed that reform in cricket administration was totally uncalled for and that everything was hunky-dory.

It is easy for those sitting cosy in the administrative 'cabal' not to endorse reform, particularly since this cabal is dominated by people who give up regular jobs to join cricket administration at the state level to eventually get to the BCCI. It enables them to continue distributing largesse to ensure that they remain in a 'vote-mustering' position. Since it is only a game of garnering votes, family members have every chance to ascend the 'throne'

---

[3]Janardhan, Arun. 'Death of a Gentleman: A Cricket Documentary Tries to Answer Hard Questions', *mint,* 29 April 2016, https://bit.ly/3eO7Zxa. Accessed on 2 September 2021.

that is vacated by their kin whether in state associations or the BCCI. There are some whose families have made it a full-time vocation merely to own and manage state associations or be office-bearers in the BCCI. They are never required to prove their mettle. If Sachin Tendulkar's son has had to demonstrate his skills to earn his spot in Mumbai's senior squad, why shouldn't an administrator's son, daughter, brother or even wife prove their capability to administer?

So what is the dominating factor that attracts whole families to the BCCI? Is it only to give Indian cricket their best? Why do people who have run state associations for upwards of 40 years want to interminably continue doing so? Do they think there is no one who can run the administration better? Do they think something about their tenure will be exposed if they quit? Why do they garner votes only for their family members to be in important positions?

After more than three years of cajoling, the state associations were finally dragged, screaming and wailing, to register their constitutions along the lines mandated by the Supreme Court. No sooner had the CoA demitted office in favour of an elected body that these associations, in the first annual general meeting (AGM), decided to recommend recall of the basic reform parameters.

Plodding through such developments, between the Supreme Court appointing the CoA and the elections being conducted as they unfolded, I examine the compulsions and the magnetic pull of the BCCI that those who are 'in' do not want to leave, ever. This is an 'insider's view' on the functioning of the BCCI.

Much has been said and written about the fact that upon joining, I had professed a 'nightwatchman' role for ourselves, but we stayed at the crease for an unduly long time.[4] Why did the

---

[4] A lower order batsman who comes higher up the order merely to shield the specialist batsman from exposure in the dying moments of the day's game.

'nightwatchman' stay on for 33 months, with neither him wanting to be at the crease for a prolonged time nor the distinguished office-bearers desiring his presence? Why did it take the CoA three years to fulfil the task assigned to it by the Supreme Court?

It is this very factor that motivated me to write this book. In explaining this issue, I am compelled to throw light on how the BCCI administers cricket in India. I reveal why Anil Kumble was given only a one-year term as coach with no clause for extension of the term[5], even when the BCCI administrators were talking about it. I explore the myth of how the BCCI supposedly lost millions of dollars they received from the ICC[6] as part of the devolution of funds among member nations. It truly was a myth around a much-touted, much-hyped model that turned out to be a mirage—a mythical formula that was never really operationalized, and delivered no revenues to the BCCI, and yet led to much backslapping.

The reader will be given a glimpse into the hiccups in playing day/night international matches and how attempts were made to disrupt the Indian cricket team's entry in the Champions Trophy 2017. I also explain why the National Cricket Academy (NCA) in Bengaluru, conceptualized as a centre of excellence and a showpiece and inaugurated in 2000, continues to be housed in the M. Chinnaswamy Stadium as a very poor cousin of the Karnataka State Cricket Association (KSCA). This is despite land being offered to the BCCI for the NCA, first in 2010 and later in 2016 by the Karnataka government.

But most importantly, I drill deeper into the incredibly bewildering reasons why state associations and the BCCI continued

---

[5]PTI. 'Anil Kumble's New Contract to Be Discussed Post Champions Trophy', *The Times of India*, 10 May 2017, https://bit.ly/3JF9AmR. Accessed on 4 January 2022.
[6]PTI. 'ICC Meet: BCCI Loses Revenue, Governance Votes as Manohar Plays Hardball', *The Times of India*, 26 April 2017, https://bit.ly/3pPmO8U. Accessed on 4 January 2022.

to oppose the Lodha reform package, which was approved by the highest court in the land.[7] On its part, the CoA, within the confines of the Supreme Court mandate, put in place an unimpeachably transparent model of governance for the BCCI. The underlying principles were transparency, professionalism and the demarcation of duties between elected office-bearers and the professional management—the bedrock of the Lodha model as approved by the Supreme Court. It also included a well-delineated accounting model and another set of guidelines for the devolution of funds.

While our mandate was to get the BCCI and the state associations to accept the new constitution, the distinguished cricket administrators suffered the continuance of the CoA since they were loath to accept the Supreme Court diktat. It sure was a perfect catch-22 situation. In fact, they had resisted the adoption of the new constitution since July 2016 and had filed innumerable interlocutory applications, all of which the Court listed for hearing. After hearing them all, it gave its final verdict in August 2018. Once again, interlocutory applications were filed. It was only in March 2019 that the Court permitted the amicus to discuss with the state associations and recommend a way forward. He held and completed his discussions by August 2019.

That cleared the path for the elections which were conducted with only three associations demurring. The elections were also an exercise in 'unanimity'. There was nothing that the electoral officer can do if the General Body (GB) comes up with a series of choices which do not trigger elections and the nominees are declared elected, uncontested.

It was highly entertaining that those very forces that had

---

[7] In January 2016, a panel headed by Justice R.M. Lodha submitted their recommendations to the apex court to overhaul the functioning of the BCCI. The Lodha panel was formed by the Supreme Court of India in 2015 in the wake of the Justice Mukul Mudgal Committee report that called for reforms within the BCCI.

been wrenched out from the BCCI by the Supreme Court and wanted to see the last of the CoA, came forth with the laughable proposal to dissolve the CoA and entrust the administration of the BCCI to a committee of former presidents. It was laughable, as these were the very office-bearers who had been disqualified by the Court.

All in all, the book contains some interesting insights into the 'calisthenics' that goes on behind the scenes in the BCCI, and how a handful of people want to continue keeping its administration captive as their cosy club. There is also a factual recounting of the scandals that have rocked the BCCI over the last decade and how every effort was made to put a lid on these scandals and save their own acts of misdemeanour.

This book is not about creating a sensation. It is not even about finding faults with people who have been in the business of administering cricket in India. It is not to cavil about how the CoA was treated. It is merely to sensitize public opinion about how much of a say the geese that lay the golden egg for the BCCI, i.e. the players, have in its affairs. Sadly, in this entire process, there is but one casualty: the players.

Through this book, I hope people will realize that cricket, which is known to be a gentleman's game, needs to be administered by gentlemen, who do their bit with sincerity, objectivity and transparency. After having done their bit, they should move on with grace and dignity, giving space to a new breed of administrators who think like the new breed of cricketers, whom they will administer. Cricket in India is religion. Cricketers are considered God. Worshippers of their God do not want the pujari (priest) to be an unwelcome broker.

I hope you enjoy reading!

1

FOUR GHOSTBUSTERS PAD UP

It was the afternoon of 30 January 2017. I was at the Indira Gandhi International Airport, Delhi, waiting to board a flight, when my phone rang. It was not a number saved on my phone. Ordinarily, I would not have picked up, but I answered thinking it may be an airline alert. The caller was Karishma Singh, a sports reporter from Times Now. Karishma mentioned that she was calling from the Supreme Court premises and that the bench headed by Justice Dipak Misra had decreed that the BCCI would be administered by a four-member CoA and I was to be the chairman of this committee. This came as a surprise to me, but Karishma insisted that she had it right.

A number of thoughts were racing through my mind, and before I had a chance to digest the information, the ever-enthusiastic Indian media had caught up with me. Navika Kumar, group editor (politics) of Times Now, was on the phone. Before I realized that our conversation was live on the channel, she started her rapid-fire questions. Not being too familiar with the goings-on in the BCCI and the Supreme Court, all I remember telling her was that it was a great honour for me to have been chosen by the Supreme Court and insisting that I saw my role in the BCCI only as a 'nightwatchman'.

The others who were announced as members of the committee were: Diana Edulji, former Indian captain and cricketing legend,

Ramachandra Guha, historian and author, whose knowledge of cricket is phenomenal, and Vikram Limaye, a banking and finance professional. The composition of the committee gave me comfort as they had been very carefully picked. The members came from diverse backgrounds but had some association with the game. If anyone at all was the rank outsider, it was me, who had had the least amount of association with contemporary cricket administration. While I had not met either Edulji or Guha, knowing that Vikram—a distinguished former colleague from the financial sector with a 'no-nonsense' disposition—was on the committee, was a source of great solace. My trepidation in getting into uncharted waters was considerably assuaged by his presence.

Obviously, the formation of the CoA was widely reported in print media the following day. However, it was the headline in *The Economic Times*—'Four Ghostbusters to Run BCCI'—that really took the cake.[1] The headline sure was intriguing but at the time I did not give it much thought. The article reported that on 30 January 2017, the Supreme Court had issued an order that the BCCI will be administered by a four-member CoA, and that the CoA was to be placed 'at the helm of the cash-rich BCCI's affairs to oversee changes to make the body more transparent and accountable'.[2]

We had to hit the ground running as a crucial ICC meeting was scheduled for 5 February and much was at stake for the BCCI in that meeting. Additionally, arrangements for the Indian Premier League (IPL) 2017 had to be put in place. Since the media was speculating over a number of issues, we scheduled an interaction

---

[1]Rautray, Samanwaya. 'Four Ghostbusters to Run BCCI', *The Economic Times*, 31 January 2017.
[2]Rautray, Samanwaya. 'Former CAG Vinod Rai to Head Administrators' Panel to Run BCCI: SC', *The Economic Times*, 31 January 2017, https://bit.ly/3pUGAzT. Accessed on 6 September 2021.

with some members of the press. I was looking forward to the interaction as I thought it would provide me with some insights from these journalists who had covered the BCCI for years.

During the course of our deliberations, a specific question asked of me was: what was the time frame you had in mind for the BCCI and the state associations to implement the Court order? My reaction was frank, and as I considered then, a forthright answer. I mentioned that we would tie it all up by October-end that year and, in any case, not go beyond 31 December 2017. The person who had asked the question had a wry smile on his face and communicated that I had more than a surprise in store for me. My feeling then was that any person or institution not obeying a diktat of the highest court in the land was totally inconceivable. In government or the civil services, the majesty of the Supreme Court has never been questioned and even a hint of contempt of court sends a chill down one's spine, so where was the question of a cricketing body not toeing the Court's line?

Nevertheless, going home after the meeting that evening, various thoughts were running through my mind about what the reporter had said. I wondered how the BCCI could take eight whole months to implement the principal order of 18 July 2016 that had handed down a direction to the Board. If the Court had given a verdict, its obedience is unquestioned. Why appoint a CoA to 'have it implemented'?

My mind went back to the headline in *The Economic Times* of 31 January. Why had the writer, Samanwaya Rautray, called the members of the committee 'ghostbusters'? We are familiar with the Ghostbusters—movies, TV series, comic books, etc. But who is a ghostbuster? A 1984 Hollywood movie by the same name has been categorized as action, comedy and fantasy. The plot follows three parapsychologists who, after having lost university funding, set up shop as a ghost-removal service in New York City that helps frightened yet sceptical customers. When I look back at our almost three-year tenure, January 2017–October 2019, I see how accurate it was: 'comedy, action and horror'! To understand this better, let me take you to 2013—when it all started.

BCCI: ON A STICKY WICKET

The BCCI has had its share of legal dalliances on which the Supreme Court has had to spend considerable time and attention.[3] However, it was in 2013, when certain allegations of spot-fixing emerged during the IPL of that year, that the Board's long and arduous journey to the apex court started.

Three players—S. Sreesanth, Ankeet Chavan and Ajit Chandila—were arrested on charges of fraud and cheating.[4] It was alleged that they were manipulating their performance in the matches to a design pre-decided with bookies. During the course of the investigations, the police found evidence of 'match-fixing' and 'spot-fixing' against some other players and arrested Gurunath Meiyappan, who happened to be closely associated with the IPL franchise Chennai Super Kings (CSK). Amongst others whose involvement was also detected was Raj Kundra, the co-owner of another franchise, Rajasthan Royals, who was also betting on IPL games. The issue drew widespread media attention because Meiyappan is the son-in-law of N. Srinivasan, the then president of the BCCI.[5]

On 26 May 2013, in an attempt to probe these allegations, the

---

[3] 'Muthiah Asks SC to Restrain BCCI Secy Srinivasan from Taking Charge as President', *The Indian Express*, 24 August 2011, https://bit.ly/3G1PUrd. Accessed on 5 January 2022.

[4] 'On This Day: Delhi Police Arrest S Sreesanth, Ankeet Chavan and Ajit Chandila in IPL Spot-Fixing Scandal', News 18, 16 May 2021, https://bit.ly/3eY9PeR. Accessed on 6 January 2022.

[5] 'CSK Owner Gurunath Meiyappan Arrested in IPL Betting Case', *The Economic Times*, 25 May 2013, https://bit.ly/3n36ZcK. Accessed on 6 January 2022.

BCCI issued a press release[6] stating that the IPL Governing Council (IPL GC) had appointed a three-member panel comprising Justice T. Jayaram Chouta, a former judge of the Karnataka and Tamil Nadu high courts, Justice R. Balasubramanian, a former judge of the Tamil Nadu High Court, and Sanjay Jagdale, secretary, BCCI. Jagdale, however, resigned from the panel. Very soon, questions about the panel's credibility were raised when news broke that the members of the IPL GC were unaware of when and how this panel had been constituted to conduct the inquiry. Instances of conflict of interest among the higher echelons of the BCCI sent out very adverse signals about the credibility of the elected office-bearers.

In June 2013, a public interest litigation (PIL) was filed by the Cricket Association of Bihar (CAB), in the Bombay High Court, challenging the constitution of the panel set up by the BCCI and the IPL GC.[7] The PIL had alleged bias by Srinivasan in constituting the probe panel as he was the president of the BCCI when the panel was formed and also the vice chairman and managing director of India Cements Limited, which owned CSK from 2008 to 2014.[8] It soon transpired during the Court hearings that Jagdale had written to Aditya Verma, secretary of the CAB, stating that he had no knowledge of an IPL GC meeting in Chennai to appoint a probe panel. Ajay Shirke, former treasurer, also informed the Court that he did not know 'who

---

[6]'Three-Member Commission to Probe Meiyappan', *The Hindu*, 27 May 2013, https://cutt.ly/RP5r5tL. Accessed on 11 February 2022.
[7]Cricket Association of Bihar (CAB) is different from Bihar Cricket Association (BCA). For more details, please refer to: ANI. 'If You Turn Blind Eye to BCA's Violation, Will Have to Approach Court: IPL Petitioner Aditya Verma to BCCI Chief', *The Times of India*, 20 September 2021, https://bit.ly/3tb18WZ. Accessed on 7 January 2022.
[8]'BCCI Panel "Illegal", against Its Own Rules: Bombay High Court', *The Times of India*, 31 July 2013, https://bit.ly/335K4Xp. Accessed on 6 January 2022.

suggested the names of the two retired judges to be appointed on the probe panel'.[9]

Meanwhile, on 28 July, the two-member probe panel, comprising the former judges, submitted its report to the BCCI working committee finding no evidence of any wrongdoing by Kundra and Meiyappan.[10] In a quick turn of events, on 30 July, a division bench of the Bombay High Court ruled that the constitution of the two-member panel, which gave a clean chit to Meiyappan and Kundra, was 'unconstitutional and illegal'.[11]

This started a long saga of legal battles into which the BCCI got dragged, besmirching its name and credibility. The situation was best described by Atul Wassan, former Test player and cricket analyst:

> To be honest, I wasn't expecting anything to come out of the inquiry. By giving them a clean chit, they are mocking the police and the judiciary. An intervention was necessary. This is the right decision taken (by some of the associations who approached the Bombay High Court). You cannot sweep everything under the carpet, just because you have control. For the BCCI this was an opportunity to send out a strong message, that they were serious about cleaning up cricket. However, they have failed to do so.[12]

Very well said! Had the issue been nipped in the bud, the IPL would have been clear of any scandals and the 'gentleman's game' would not have lost its fair reputation.

---

[9] Gollapudi, Nagaraj. 'Letters Reveal Panel Appointment Process Flawed', *ESPN crickinfo*, 30 July 2013, https://es.pn/3sZ1jEr. Accessed on 5 September 2021.
[10] 'Investigation Finds "No Wrongdoing" by IPL Owners', *ESPN crickinfo*, 28 July 2013, https://es.pn/3EXmhWz. Accessed on 6 January 2022.
[11] Khushboo Narayan and Gouri Shah. 'BCCI's Panel Probing IPL Spot Fixing Illegal, Says Court', *mint*, 3 August 2013, https://bit.ly/32RXciY. Accessed on 6 January 2022.
[12] Ibid.

SUPREME COURT ENTERS THE ARENA

The Bombay High Court order was neither acceptable to the BCCI nor to the CAB. Both rushed to the Supreme Court. On 5 August, the BCCI filed a special leave petition (SLP) in the Supreme Court challenging the Bombay High Court order and sought the setting up of a Special Purpose Committee (SPC) comprising two independent persons to examine if further probe was required into all the issues mentioned in the charge sheet filed by the Mumbai Police. The CAB, too, approached the Court challenging the high court's order in refusing to appoint a fresh committee to probe the scam. It pleaded that when the high court had declared the panel of two judges as unconstitutional, it should have appointed a fresh committee to look into the issue.

On 7 October, the Supreme Court bench of Justice(s) Jagdish Singh Khehar and A.K. Patnaik, rejecting both the pleas, ordered the setting up of an independent three-member panel to probe the allegation of betting and spot-fixing. The panel, headed by Justice Mukul Mudgal, former Chief Justice of the Punjab and Haryana High Court, also included then additional solicitor general of India, L. Nageswara Rao, and senior advocate and member of the Assam Cricket Association (ACA), Nilay Dutta. The bench said that the panel would conduct an independent inquiry into the allegations and submit its report to the Supreme Court in four months' time. It permitted the Mumbai Police to conduct an independent investigation and submit its findings separately to the Court.

The Mudgal panel's first report was submitted in February 2014. Its finding was that, Meiyappan and Kundra had indulged in betting.[13] The panel also submitted a sealed envelope, meant to

---

[13] Kumar, K.C. Vijaya. 'A Saga of Shame and Intrigue', *The Hindu*, 15 July 2015, https://bit.ly/3EXpB3Z. Accessed on 6 January 2022.

be opened by the judges only, containing the names of persons who were allegedly involved in fraud associated with the game. The Court asked Srinivasan to step down from the presidency of the BCCI to allow for a fair investigation of the scandal and directed the panel to continue its investigation, particularly against the persons mentioned in the sealed envelope.

In November 2014, the Court permitted the Mudgal committee report, dealing with the role of four individuals—Srinivasan, Kundra, Sundar Raman (then chief operating officer [COO] of the IPL) and Meiyappan—who were under the committee's scanner, to be given to the persons in question and the BCCI for their respective rejoinders.[14] Although the Court did not hold Srinivasan guilty of either betting or fixing, it held that he had known of an IPL player violating the code but had taken no action. It also held that Raman had known a bookie and had contacted him eight times that season.[15] The Court took serious note of a recommendation in the Mudgal panel report which stated:

> Most of the persons who were not connected with BCCI pointed out the issue of conflict of interest brought about by the ownership of Chennai Super Kings by India Cement, a company whose Managing Director Mr. N. Srinivasan, the current President of BCCI was. It was also pointed out that the conflict of interest was brought about by the amendment to clause 6.2.4 of the BCCI Rules and Regulations by which an office bearer of BCCI was permitted to hold a commercial interest in the IPL and Champions League. The

---

[14] 'SC Names Srinivasan in Spot Fixing Probe', *The Assam Tribune*, 15 September 2010, https://bit.ly/3t25PC4. Accessed on 6 January 2022.

[15] Mathur, Aneesha. 'Mudgal Report: IPL Top Boss Named for "Bookie Links", N Srinivasan Gets a Slap on the Wrist', *The Indian Express*, 18 November 2014, https://bit.ly/3q0DVEW. Accessed on 6 January 2022.

above amendment was the subject matter of a petition in the Supreme Court leading to a split verdict by two Judges, but the issue now stands unresolved due to the withdrawal of the proceedings which led to the above petition in the Supreme Court by Shri A.C. Muthiah, a former president of BCCI.

The issue of conflict of interest is Mr. N. Srinivasan being the BCCI President and CEO (chief executive officer) of India Cement has been raised by several persons who are neither in the BCCI hierarchy nor are beneficiaries of BCCI.

While it is evident that the questions raised before us about conflict of interest are serious and may have large scale ramifications on the functioning of cricket, we do not deem it proper to pronounce our opinion on this issue as it is not directly in our terms of reference. However, since several stakeholders repeatedly stressed on this issue, we thought it proper to bring this issue to the attention of this Hon'ble Court.[16]

To appreciate the developments which followed, it is necessary to understand why conflict of interest has taken centre stage in the functioning of the BCCI and how it took birth. The original clause in the BCCI's Rules and Regulations (2008) read as: 'No administrator shall have, directly or indirectly, any commercial interest in the matches and events conducted by the Board.'

This clause was amended, in what is alleged to be in a hurried manner, to the following: 'Clause 6.2.4: No administrator shall have directly or indirectly any commercial interest in the matches or events conducted by the Board, excluding events like IPL or champions League twenty 20'.

This amendment was clearly a blatant instance of conflict of interest.

---

[16]Justice Mudgal IPL Probe Committee, 'A Report on the Allegations of Betting and Spot/Match Fixing in the Indian Premier League-Season 6', Volume 1.

In January 2015, the Court finally applied itself to the conflict of interest aspect. In its order, the Court held the rule to be 'void and ineffective' and 'unsustainable and impermissible in law' since it had 'authorized' the 'creation and continuation' of a conflict of interest situation. In a further comment made by the bench comprising Justice(s) T.S. Thakur and F.M.I. Kalifulla, it maintained that the rule was the 'true villain' in having perpetuated the conflict as it had led to 'three real life situations' of conflict of interest due to Srinivasan's dual roles. In considerable attention paid to this issue, the Court listed such situations:

1. The first instance arose when the BCCI awarded compensation of a sum of ₹10.40 crore to CSK, on account of the cancellation of the Champions League Twenty20 (CLT20) Tournament 2008. A similar amount was awarded to Rajasthan Royals, the other finalist.[17] However, since Srinivasan had participated in the deliberations leading to the decision, it could be alleged that he was privy to a self-serving decision that benefited India Cements Ltd, a company promoted by him. Even though a few others, as members of IPL GC, also participated in the decision-making process, it still does not cure the legal flaw arising out of the fact that the benefactor was also the beneficiary of the decision.
2. The second instance saw the light when an award of a sum of ₹13.10 crore came in the year 2009, pertaining to the same cancellation of the CLT20, 2008, against unaudited claims of loss by CSK and Rajasthan Royals. This too fell afoul of his duty, on the one hand, and interest on the other. Kapil Sibal, appearing for India Cements, argued

---

[17]Garodia, Sunil. 'Much Needed Check on BCCI', *The Statesman*, 19 February 2015, https://bit.ly/3FZsUcr. Accessed on 6 January 2022.

that this amount was returned by ICL subsequently,[18] but the return did not improve matters. The decision to award an amount higher than the one awarded earlier appears to have led to public criticism, raising the pitch further for Srinivasan's removal from the BCCI on the grounds of conflict of interest. Return of the amount because of a public outcry may, no doubt, mean that Mr Srinivasan tried to come clean on the subject even when his company may have suffered a loss. However, it may also mean that the return of the amount came only under public pressure and in recognition of the fact that the amount was not actually due and payable and yet was paid to the detriment of the BCCI, a trustee of general public interest in the sport of cricket and everything that goes with it.

3. The third instance where Srinivasan's commercial interest came in direct conflict with his duty as president of the BCCI was when allegations of betting were levelled against his son-in-law, Gurunath Meiyappan. That being so, a clear conflict of interest, the Court observed, had arisen between what is Srinivasan's duty as president of the BCCI and his loyalty as father-in-law as well as the owner of team CSK on the other.[19]

With these observations, the Court struck down the controversial amendment which had permitted BCCI officials to have a commercial interest in the IPL and the CLT20. Not being content with the order, the Board moved a review petition

---

[18]Civil Appeal No. 4235 of 2014, Indian Kanoon, https://indiankanoon.org/doc/194744123/. Accessed on 14 February 2022.
[19]Civil Appeal No. 4235 of 2014 read with CA 4236 of 2014 with 1155 of 2015 delivered on 22 January 2015, Indian Kanoon, https://indiankanoon.org/doc/194744123/. Accessed on 14 February 2022.

against this January 2015 verdict which too was rejected on 29 September 2015. It then moved a curative petition. The Court dismissed that too, saying: 'We have gone through the curative petition and the relevant documents. In our opinion, no case is made out... Hence, the curative petition is dismissed', a bench comprising Chief Justice T.S. Thakur and Justice(s) J.S. Khehar and Dipak Misra ordered.[20]

The Supreme Court, in January that year, ordered the constitution of a committee of three former judges of the Supreme Court headed by former Chief Justice R.M. Lodha. The committee had the following mandate:

1. Determine the punishment to be awarded to Meiyappan, Kundra and their franchises.
2. Examine the role of Sundar Raman, and if found guilty, impose a suitable punishment.
3. Recommend reforms in the practices and procedures of the BCCI and also amendments in the Memorandum of Association and Rules and Regulations.

The Lodha Committee, empowered with the order of the Supreme Court, conducted a very detailed questioning and investigation of the entire episode. It was assisted by lawyers and investigating officers. In its first findings delivered in July 2015, declaring that the spirit of cricket is larger than any individual, their cricket franchises or financial losses, it ordered the suspension of CSK and Rajasthan Royals from the IPL for a period of two years. The committee, however, permitted the players of the two teams to be auctioned off to other franchises.

The Committee suspended Meiyappan and Kundra from any

---

[20]Rajagopal, Krishnadas. 'BCCI Curative Petition against Conflict of Interest Verdict Dismissed', *The Hindu*, 17 December 2016, https://cutt.ly/UP5toFQ. Accessed on 14 September 2022.

and all involvement with the BCCI for life.[21] The two team officials found guilty of betting by the Supreme Court were also suspended from taking part in any cricketing activities for a maximum of five years. It was observed that this was being ordered to safeguard the purity of the game as the controversy had shaken the foundations of cricket.

I have discussed in detail the findings of the Supreme Court and the two panels set up by it to establish the concern that was being expressed in the media and all cricketing circles about the erosion in the credibility of the BCCI due to widespread allegations of conflict of interest and the fact that the BCCI had become a captive of a close set of interests. Nothing sums up the public perception following the court verdict better than this newspaper report:

> The BCCI has for long operated as a privileged and closed club. By involving leaders from most political parties, it has ensured that it did not fall foul of the administration. A closed set of people have been taking decisions which smack of arbitrariness without actually breaching any law. It has resisted attempts to bring it under the Right to Information Act (RTI).[22]

More need not be said.

LODHA COMMITTEE BATS FOR REFORM

The Lodha Committee recommendations were presented on 4 January 2016. It recommended a complete overhaul of

---

[21] Deepalakshmi, K. 'IPL Scam: Lodha Panel Suspends CSK, RR Franchises for Two Years', *The Hindu*, 30 August 2016, https://bit.ly/3ztpcVU. Accessed on 5 September 2021.
[22] Garodia, Sunil. 'Much Needed Check on BCCI', *The Statesman*, 19 February 2015, https://bit.ly/3FZsUcr. Accessed on 5 September 2021.

Indian cricket—from the highest echelons comprising elected office-bearers to the playing level. It sought a reform among all the stakeholders. It was clear from the Committee's report that its recommendations were aimed at taking on the established order in the BCCI. In its opening chapter, the Committee commented that ills had become endemic due to the apathy of high functionaries in the BCCI, some of who had been in-charge of the state associations for decades. It also observed that policies had been formulated to suit powerful interests and the highest court in the land had found that the game had fallen into disrepute.[23]

The Committee suggested sweeping reforms and recommended a new constitution for the BCCI with the intent of providing a corporate structure capable of handling the complexities that the cricket administration was facing. It proposed a 'one-state, one-vote policy'—one cricket association, having full-time membership and voting rights in the BCCI, in one state. It also proposed a three-tier structure—the GB, the Apex Council (Board of Directors) at the helm to provide policy directions and professional managers or whole-time employees who would be responsible for the day-to-day management under a CEO. The Committee also recommended the setting up of a separate cricket players' association for former male and female cricketers.

Reform is not necessarily a good word. It is indeed a very unacceptable term for the interested few, whom it seeks to reform. Sweeping reforms get the worse reception. It sweeps away those very people who do not desire to be swept aside. It uproots people with deep roots. It messes with a cosy set-up which serves the people who operate it. The longer they have operated that system, the more they are entrenched in it and the better they can argue for their indispensability. They canvass experience, they

---

[23]Report of the Supreme Court Committee on Reforms in Cricket [Volume One–Report & Annexures], 18 December 2015.

canvass continuity, and above all feel that courts and governments have no place on their 'playground'. They become masters of the 22 yards. The Lodha Committee report got the same reception.

There was an orchestrated chorus: how could the principle of 'one-state, one-vote' operate? Associations like Vadodara (Baroda) and Mumbai had, between them, won the Ranji Trophy for more than half the times, so how can they be ignored? How could cricket be run by just three selectors? Beyond these two aspects, protests on grounds of principle vanished. What came into play was personal interest: objections to the age limit of 70 for elected office-bearers, 'cooling-off' after three years and the nine-year limit on being an office-bearer in state associations and the BCCI. But these reform suggestions had not become law as yet. The Court gave the BCCI time till 31 January 2016 for suggestions. No suggestions came. The apex court then gave them time till 3 March 2016.

In March 2016, the BCCI, in a 55-page counter affidavit, stated that whilst it had accepted some of the reforms, it had concerns on many of the recommendations presented by the Lodha Committee. The BCCI maintained that the recommendations were impractical and may lead to corruption and inequality. The basic objection was to the 'one-state, one-vote' principle. It was felt that it would lead to corruption as had been seen in Fédération Internationale de Football Association (FIFA).[24] It was contended that the BCCI membership structure is historically based on levels of cricketing activity rather than geographical limits of the states, which are merely political subdivisions created on linguistic basis much after the BCCI was formally established in 1929. Further, it was asserted that it was unjust to limit appointments based on a person's age

---

[24]Rajagopal, Krishnadas. 'BCCI Presents Its Counters to Most Major Lodha Panel Recommendations', *The Hindu*, 3 March 2016, https://bit.ly/31tJaDp. Accessed on 6 January 2022.

or the number of years they had served in the organization. The BCCI argued that the recommendation restricted the members the freedom of their association with the organization. It was also felt that its strength was in the continuity of its meritorious administrators. It was argued that these were the people who ensured the BCCI's strength and importance in the cricket world. Similarly, the bar on ministers, government officials and persons holding honorary posts was a restriction on their constitutional freedom granted under Article (19)(1)(c). The affidavit also claimed that having a nominee of the comptroller and auditor general of India (CAG) on the Apex Council would be contrary to law and an infliction of governmental interference in an autonomous body. Thus, in totality, the affidavit objected to almost all the major recommendations of the Committee.

The BCCI's opposition to the reform package was so severe that it forced the bench, in its hearing of April 2016, to ask the then attorney representing the BCCI if 'the BCCI was refusing to reform'. The BCCI maintained that it was a private body which could arrange its matters in any way it deemed fit and that memberships were part of internal management. In case of complaints, they approach the registrar of cooperative societies, or police stations, or the court. There had been no instance of malfeasance to trigger interference, thus changing the very character and functioning of the Board. Though the BCCI had objected to a CAG nominee being on its Apex Council, it, had no objection if a minister was to be elected to it.

Delivering its final verdict on 18 July 2016, the Supreme Court accepted the major recommendations of the Lodha Committee, including a ban on ministers and civil servants and those above 70 from becoming the Board's members and each state was granted only one vote in the elections. No person could hold more than three three-year terms as a BCCI official, and no official could serve consecutive terms. The Court also accepted the recommendation to have a CAG nominee on the Apex Council of the BCCI. The Court, however, left it to Parliament to decide whether the BCCI should come under RTI and whether betting on the game should be legalized. The Court finally went on to maintain that: 'The inherent constitution of the BCCI is such that it is highly incapable of achieving the values of transparency, objectivity and accountability such that without changing its structure it can't be done so.'[25] It gave the BCCI time up to six months to implement the recommendations and appointed Justice Lodha to oversee the transition.

To an ordinary citizen, an order of the Supreme Court is '*Lakshman Rekha*'—a final word; there is no question of disobeying it. All of us who have been in government would baulk at the very thought of defying a high court order, let alone even conceive of taking on the apex court of the country. This somehow does not apply to the BCCI. After all, the Court had raised the very issues that were agitating minds in the BCCI. These issues had become anathema to the select few who were holding the BCCI captive in this millennium and had caused them to take on the Court so aggressively.

In a Special General Meeting (SGM) convened in October 2016, the BCCI rejected some of the key recommendations aimed at administrative reform. It rejected the 'one-state, one-vote' rule, the age limit of 70 years and the cooling-off period of three years.[26] It was decided in the SGM to draw up a detailed report to be presented to the Supreme Court explaining why they were rejecting the Lodha Panel clauses. This was after having missed the 30 September deadline for implementing the reforms. It was

---

[25]PTI. 'BCCI Constitution Incapable of Achieving Transparency: SC', *The Times of India*, 3 May 2016, https://bit.ly/3n09gpi. Accessed on 5 September 2021.
[26]PTI. 'BCCI Refuses to Budge, Rejects Key Lodha Committee Recommendations in SGM', *Firstpost*, 1 October 2016, https://cutt.ly/bP5tnIX. Accessed on 5 September 2021.

also decided to disburse ₹16.72 crore each to 13 state associations. However, in a short interim order passed on 7 October 2016, the Court directed the associations to freeze the funds received by them till they agreed to the reforms. The Court directed the associations to file their affidavits by 17 October, when the case was slated for hearing again and even cautioned: 'Do not precipitate matters'.[27]

None of these warnings seemed to matter to the BCCI and it continued its recalcitrance forcing the Lodha Panel, in its next status report, to request the Court to dismiss the top brass of the BCCI and automatically remove all the office-bearers of the state associations that had not adopted the criteria set by the top court in July. It then sought the Court's permission to appoint G.K. Pillai, former Union home secretary, as an observer, to monitor the administration of the Board.

However, totally indifferent to the Lodha Panel filing this status report, the BCCI, in its SGM convened in November 2016, decided to stick to its decision taken by the SGM on 1 October. Only three associations—Hyderabad, Vidarbha and Tripura—had agreed to implement the recommendations in full while the others had rejected it.

With this defiance of court directions, the BCCI was certainly risking the wrath of the Court in the hearing scheduled on 5 December. The Court was aghast at the intransigence of the BCCI and decided to post the case for final hearing on 2 January 2017 to consider the recommendations made by the Lodha Panel on the dismissal of the BCCI office-bearers and appointment of an observer.

The BCCI had taken a very rigid stand. Whilst it continued

---

[27]PTI. 'SC Directs BCCI Not to Give Funds to States Averse to Reforms', *Business Standard*, 7 October 2016, https://bit.ly/3G2LGzx. Accessed on 5 September 2021.

arguing in public that the Lodha recommendations were impractical and difficult to implement, possibly the only ground on which it had a principled stance was that of 'one state, one vote'. Maybe there was another matter of practical difficulty—of having only three selectors against the five that it usually retained. This practical difficulty resided in the fact that the BCCI conducts, besides international games, about 2,000 domestic matches. It is practically difficult for three selectors to cover these matches to get an idea of the talent available. The opposition to the other recommendations, which, in a manner of speaking, had got the BCCI's goat—the tenure, the age limit and the 'cooling-off' clauses—were on personal grounds and not a matter of principle. It needs to be recognized that the forces that these clauses were effecting certainly were strong enough for the office-bearers to risk contempt of court, but not budge on their defiant stand.

With all the annoyance displayed by the Court in its last three hearings, the BCCI still had not considered it prudent to withdraw from its arrogant and aggressive stand and accept the reform package, seeking maybe one or two modifications to its earlier judgment (which the Court might have permitted). All cricket enthusiasts and followers of the game have wondered at the magnetic forces that compel people to stick to power. Why was it that they could not say 'enough' and take a back seat or an emeritus position and let younger and sprightlier minds take over? Just because they have the capacity to garner votes, they desire to hold the administration of the game captive to their whims.

The axe had to fall and fall it did. For any country, the majesty of its apex court cannot be tampered with. It was probably for the love of the game that the lordships did not order contempt of court proceedings on the office-bearers. In its sitting on 2 January 2017, the Court ordered the removal of the president, Anurag Thakur, and secretary, Ajay Shirke, from their respective posts for not complying with its order to implement administrative reforms within the body. The Court also directed that other office-bearers who did not meet the eligibility criteria fixed in its 18 July order should cease to hold office immediately. The senior-most vice president was C.K. Khanna and he was thus mandated to function as the acting president, and the joint secretary, Amitabh Choudhary, to be the acting secretary.

The order served to be the culmination of a process that had started after the Court's verdict of 18 July 2016, accepting the Lodha Panel recommendation and ordering the BCCI to take steps to adopt the new constitution. The Court ordered that a committee of administrators would be appointed to supervise the functioning of the BCCI through its CEO. Thus entered the CoA.

While delivering its verdict, the Court observed:

> The course of events indicates that though sufficient opportunities have been granted to BCCI to comply with the judgment and order of this Court, it has failed to do so. The President and Secretary and office bearers of BCCI have obstructed the implementation of the final directions of this Court on the basis of a specious plea that its State Associations are not willing to abide by the directions. This Court having furnished sufficient opportunities to BCCI to comply, it is constrained now to take recourse to coercive steps to ensure that the directions contained in its final judgment and order are not left to be a writ in sand.[28]

Strong words by the Court. It would ring alarm bells for a normal person, and cause sleepless nights. But not for the BCCI.

---

[28] 'Supreme Court Removes Thakur, Shirke from Top BCCI Posts', *ESPN crickinfo*, 2 January 2017, https://es.pn/3G2iicT. Accessed on 5 September 2021.

COA: 22 YARDS BECKON

On 30 January, the Court announced the names of the members of the CoA and inter alia ordered: 'The CEO of BCCI shall report to the Committee of Administrators and the Administrators shall supervise the management of BCCI...'[29]

The issues arising from the court order that needed to be taken note of are:

1. The CoA shall supervise the administration of the BCCI through its CEO.
2. The CoA shall also ensure that the directions, contained in the judgment of the Court dated 18 July 2016 are fulfilled.
3. The office-bearers were to function subject to the supervision and control of the CoA.
4. The administrators shall supervise the management of the BCCI.

The point that needs to be emphasized is that the role of the CoA was twofold: first, to ensure the implementation of the 18 July order of the Court, that is, to have the constitution adopted and second, to supervise the management of the BCCI.

I have laboured this point because quite often the CoA has been questioned for interfering with the management of the BCCI when that was not its role. If that had not been its role, the CoA would not have waded into the issue of discussing financial models with the ICC or even taken control and ensured that IPL 2017 actually took place since all forces were aligned towards ensuring disruption!

The takeaway from this long narrative is that, had the BCCI

---

[29]The Supreme Court Appointed Committee of Administrators of the BCCI, Directions Issued by the Committee of Administrators on Selection Committee Meeting.

been transparent and a cricket body run solely for the development of cricket in the country, its office-bearers would have set aside their personal agenda and agreed to an independent inquiry the moment the IPL match-fixing/betting/conflict-of-interest issues arose in 2013. There were enough adverse comments on those at the helm of the BCCI in the reports of the Mudgal and Lodha committees.

If those against whom comments were made had the grace, they would have stepped aside and permitted other equally experienced and professionally capable people to manage the Board. Even if comments of these two committees did not indicate the writing on the wall, the 18 July 2016 judgment was a message—as loud and clear as it can be—that their days were over. Not acting with grace, dignity and objectivity caused all this pain to the BCCI as well as cricket in India and exposed the real intentions and motivations of those who were holding the BCCI captive.

After getting acquainted with the functioning of the BCCI, it became very clear to me that the observations of the Court were indeed spot on. The BCCI did suffer from a total lack of objectivity, transparency and professionalism. How do you run a body with a budget of about ₹10,000 crore without a chief financial officer (CFO) or CEO? It possibly suited the interests of the elected office-bearers to have part-time elected members manage day-to-day administration and finance. While it suited their interests, it was a huge disservice to the cricket administration and created legal and administrative complications for the BCCI.

Clearly, there was a lot that the CoA had to deal with as it prepared to oversee the administration of the BCCI.

2

TAKING GUARD IN THE BCCI

The task early in the innings was for all four of us to get on the same wavelength, build consensus amongst ourselves and approach issues with an integrated mindset. Even though two amongst us had been close to the game and had multifarious connections in the cricketing community, there was no opportunity for us to bring forth our proclivities, or for that matter, of some other cricketing personality, who had a particular viewpoint and had not been able to convince the BCCI to conform to it. Already, various disgruntled cricketers and journalists were attempting to use us as instruments to enforce their angularities.

Each one of us got numerous mails every day from disgruntled/side-lined/renegade/opinionated cricketers and cricket administrators. There was no scope to have CoA meetings conform to one viewpoint as the *only* course of action. Even if it was the right course of action, it was extremely early to start thrusting individual viewpoints as the committee's consensus. In any case, it was extremely presumptuous for any CoA member to start thinking that it was 'my way or the highway'.

Our priority task was to ensure that we conduct the IPL, as those who had been ousted from administration had taken the stand: 'no IPL without us'. IPL 2017 was successfully organized against heavy odds. In doing so, there was no scope for anyone of us to let our own personal opinions around the format become supercilious over majority consensus.

It was also too early for us to sweep away all the so-called 'bad and ugly' practices plaguing Indian cricket, just within a few months of our appointment. We are all aware of the 'superstar' culture in cricket. There are self-styled VIP cricket administrators who strut around as if they own the BCCI, nay Indian cricket itself. They had to be disabused of that notion. The culture had to be changed. What we recognized was that it had grown in the organization over at least four decades. It could not be erased with one press statement or diktat.

We also recognized our mandate clearly: to persuade the BCCI and its constituent associations to accept the court direction viz. the Lodha recommendations. Even though the boundaries within which the CoA was to fulfil its mandate were well defined, interested elements have repeatedly faulted us for straying into the administration of the BCCI. Such observations have been trotted out to create the impression that the Supreme Court entrusted the CoA with the mandate of making the states adopt the new constitution and wanted the officiating office-bearers to *continue* running the day-to-day administration of the BCCI. Though clarified umpteen times, the misinformation was spread to suit the interests of the persons who wanted their writ to run by remote control.

Whilst the mandate to ensure the implementation of the 18 July judgment was definitely the core issue for the CoA, it could not preside over the slipshod management of an administratively and financially opaque organization. It was incumbent upon the CoA to draft a set of administrative and financial guidelines to establish a governance structure that is systematic and orderly.

It must be said to the credit of the Lodha Committee that the architecture of the governance structure that they recommended for the BCCI was exceedingly well-thought-out and systematically designed. It was conceptualized on the design of a corporate entity with the magnitude of scale as the budget of the BCCI would require.

The structure was a three-tier set-up. At the helm was obviously the GB, which would elect six members to the nine-member Apex Council (six elected and three nominated). The Apex Council was akin to the Board of Directors of a company as it was designed to give strategic guidance, provide policy guidelines and oversight, and hold the management accountable for its actions. It was empowered to control the finances of the BCCI, regulate player-related issues (foreign tours, payments and allowances, and domestic tournaments) and frame rules regarding appointment and conditions of service of all employees.

At the third tier, day-to-day management functions were meant to be undertaken by professionals in all cricketing and non-cricketing matters. For example, the management of non-cricketing matters including operations, human resources (HR), finance and media was to be conducted by the CEO under the supervision of the Apex Council. The CEO was to be assisted by professionals performing specialized functions (HR, finance, media, etc.). Cricketing matters such as selections and coaching evaluation were to be managed by cricket committees. This three-tier structure is ideal for the efficient and systematic functioning of the BCCI.

GETTING OUR EYE IN

An important component of this structure was a full-time CEO. But the BCCI did not have a regular CEO or CFO—a major lacuna which was widely commented upon in all orders of the Court. This was starkly in contrast to other prominent boards, such as those of Australia and England, which have a full-time professional CEO.[30] Invariably, these are former cricketers who have played and understood the game and its administration. For the BCCI, a full-time CEO and CFO were appointed in 2016 at the behest of the Court. The elected part-time president and secretary had been happy to discharge the role of chief executive. Those interested in retaining the status quo ante in the administration of the BCCI have often argued that it is the best-run sports entity. While it may be true or otherwise, I do not want to enter into any dispute on that aspect.

However, not having any experienced professional run the administration causes some irritants of the kind that were experienced in 2016. One such irritant/ambiguity had crept into the appointment letter of the CEO. Rahul Johri was appointed as the CEO that year, and his appointment letter was signed by the then president of the BCCI. It included a clause to regulate his increments. It took the BCCI/CoA two years to interpret that clause. The learned amicus curiae opined on it. Diana had obtained an independent interpretation from a retired judge. The BCCI legal team had also accessed external legal opinion. As it turned out, both interpretations were diametrically opposite to each other. Finally, an interpretation emerged around which consensus could not be built. A full-time professional CEO/CFO could have ensured that such ambiguities do not occur.

The other case was the appointment of a security advisor. His appointment order did not mention either the tenure of his office or his age of retirement. Such lacunae were cause of avoidable dissonance among the officials.

The BCCI has an interesting tradition of the elected office-bearers having a couple of persons helping them at their place of

---

[30]Cricket Australia (CA) has had a full-time CEO since its inception in 1892. The England and Wales Cricket Board (ECB) also got a CEO after the different boards merged to create the ECB in 1997.

residence. There could be two persons stationed at home and an executive assistant (EA), who would be available to them at all times. The EA also travelled with them, within and outside the country. These employees were appointed entirely at the pleasure of the office-bearers. There was no due process for selection. All that was required was that the office-bearer provides the name, designation and salary of the person that the BCCI should employ as their EA or personal staff. That is enough for the person to receive an appointment letter. The BCCI, sometimes, never saw some of these people's faces, even though they were on its payroll.

The intriguing part was that when the tenure of the office-bearers who were functioning alongside the CoA was terminated with the election of the new office-bearers, the EAs working with them claimed to be permanent employees of the BCCI and demanded to continue in their roles. The appointment letter was also indicative of them being taken on the payroll of the BCCI, despite the selection not being against any permanent vacancy, no advertisement calling for applications or any due process followed for selection.

Another remarkable case which is certainly going to cause substantial financial loss relates to payment of stamp duty on contracts. As per the advice of elected office-bearers, since the rate of stamp duty applicable in Maharashtra was high, copies of all contracts entered into by the BCCI were kept in Delhi and stamp duty paid as per rates prevailing in Delhi. In their wisdom, the BCCI had bundled all contract documents in steel boxes and kept them at hired premises in Delhi to supposedly avoid paying higher rate of tax applicable in Maharashtra.[31]

Soon, the BCCI received a notice from the Collector of Stamps, Mumbai, seeking details of all contracts entered into

---

[31] Minutes of the meeting of the CoA, 12 April 2017, BCCI, https://cutt.ly/aP5tCxd. Accessed on 14 February 2022.

by it, irrespective of where the contract had been signed. The collector levied tax amounting to about ₹100 crore. The CoA was aghast to learn of this and in its meeting on 21 April 2017, apprised the office-bearers of the new liability, requesting them to decide on the issue of pending stamp duty on old contracts to avoid further embarrassment.

These issues point to the non-existence of a system or standard operating procedure (SOP) by which routine administrative concerns are carried out in any organization. It is thus no surprise that the Justice Lodha Committee compelled the BCCI to appoint a full-time CEO.

The CoA was also cognizant of the fact that the BCCI had been captive to issues like nepotism and misuse of insider information; these were possibly the notoriously dominating factors necessitating the entry of the Supreme Court. It was also captive to ad hoc policies and procedures. There were disputes and litigations galore as decisions to include/exclude IPL teams had been taken to suit various dispensations then dominant in the BCCI. This led to multiple disputes with vendors, business partners and stakeholders. There have been arbitration awards which have gone against the institution, such as the termination of the IPL team Kochi Tuskers Kerala, which could have cost the organization ₹1,700 crore.[32]

The Kochi Tuskers Kerala case is a typical case displaying total lack of any standards of governance. To provide context, the Kochi team was terminated by the BCCI in 2011, citing breach of franchise agreement and their bank guarantee of ₹153 crore was encashed. Following the termination, the franchise went to court, demanding ₹350 crore as compensation from the BCCI. The

---

[32] B., Ventaka Krishna. 'SC Orders BCCI to Cough Up Rs 1,700 Cr for Kochi Tuskers', *The New Indian Express*, 16 March 2018, https://bit.ly/3HLp9rI. Accessed on 31 August 2021.

court ordered arbitration by a former Chief Justice of India (CJI), which was duly undertaken. The verdict went against the BCCI, who were ordered to pay, with effect from September 2011, ₹385 crore as damages, in addition to the encashed bank guarantee, which amounted to ₹540 crore with 18 per cent annual penalty.

The BCCI, clearly dissatisfied with the award, approached the Supreme Court, which in turn upheld the arbitral award and directed them to pay the amount with the aforementioned annual interest, which amounted to ₹1,700 crore. In October 2017, the IPL GC chairman and office-bearers negotiated with the franchise to arrive at a decision mutually beneficial to both parties. The agreement that they arrived at was to settle for ₹850 crore plus simple interest at 9 per cent.[33]

The GC decided to place the matter in the GB meeting with a recommendation to accept the offer. Umpteen GB meetings have been held since then. The members have been more anxious in seeking a reversal of the Supreme Court-mandated constitution than take a view on this settlement. It will make interesting reading to see how much the BCCI is ultimately made to fork out. There is also the exclusion of the Deccan Chargers, the arbitration award of which has also gone against the BCCI. The award has been set aside by the Mumbai High Court. It has to be seen if the aggrieved party will appeal.

SCORING BIG WITH REFORM

Besides the fact that there was a total lack of transparency in making decisions regarding vendors, player selection and appointment of officials, there was no semblance of an oversight mechanism. The central concern expressed in all the observations of the Court was

---

[33]Minutes of the meeting of the CoA, 24–25 October 2017, BCCI, https://cutt.ly/9P5t1SG. Accessed on 14 February 2022.

that the BCCI was not being professionally run, its governance suffered from a lack of accountability and transparency, and that conflict of interest was rampant among all its office-bearers. Justice Lodha had commented:

> We found that the time has come that the BCCI should be run professionally, it should not have any monopoly of a family or of an individual. There should be full transparency in its action, the office bearers must be accountable and there should be good governance and the day-to-day management should be in the hands of professionals and that has been accepted by the Supreme Court.[34]

In view of the concern expressed by the Court regarding transparency and professionalism in the BCCI, the first thing that the CoA, a court-mandated body, decided was to address these deficiencies in the administration of the BCCI and ensure transparency in all its operations.

The BCCI does not want to call itself a public institution. It has taken the position in all courts that it is a private body, and hence it does not come within the mandate of the RTI or the Central Information Commission. For the sake of argument, let us assume that we accept this stance. The fact remains that the team it fields is known as 'Team India' and that it is the only entity that conducts the *Indian* Premier League. It is thus incumbent upon the BCCI to keep cricket enthusiasts apprised of how its decisions are being taken and how it collects and spends its money.

In the process of doing so, the CoA decided to upgrade the BCCI website by making it more interactive and user-friendly. A

---

[34]Kotian, Harish. 'There Should Be Full Transparency in the BCCI's Actions: Justice Lodha', *Rediff.com*, 2 January 2017, https://cutt.ly/NP5t6yG. Accessed on 14 February 2022.

new website was created, with increased emphasis on openness and accountability. Through this medium, all our activities and decisions were to be put in the public domain. The idea was to provide transparency to all actions, decisions and expenditures undertaken by the CoA. The CoA decided to post the minutes of all its meetings on the website. It also proposed to put in public domain all the references that it was making to the Supreme Court.

All expenses exceeding ₹25 lakh were also to be posted on the website. This decision of the CoA met with huge appreciation from all parties of interest in cricket in the country, as evident from the extract that appeared when the CoA demitted office:

> ...Recently it submitted the 11th Status Report... Apart from the CoA documentation, details of membership of the State Associations, amicus curiae documentation... and more recently from the Electoral Officer's office were also posted on the BCCI website... The Indian Cricketers' Association (ICA) website also became a useful source of information.[35]

FILLING IN THE GAPS IN PLAYERS' COMPENSATION

The BCCI is believed to be the richest cricketing body in the world. How has it become this rich? Its riches have obviously accrued due to the fame of its cricketers and the immense global viewership of the matches they play. The BCCI rakes in revenue only because Indian cricketers have worldwide appeal. The CoA learned, much to its astonishment, that the BCCI had not revised the compensation package of its contracted players since 2011. The contracts for players and support staff for 2016–17 had not

---

[35] Vishwanath, G. 'CoA Documentation: A Good Practice the New BCCI Set-Up Could Follow', *Sportstar*, 16 October 2019, https://bit.ly/3HCA8Dw. Accessed on 31 August 2021.

been concluded when the CoA took charge on 30 January 2017. This was certainly unpardonable.

Hastening to remedy this unconscionable treatment, after obtaining the advice of experienced administrators such as Prof. Ratnakar Shetty and Dr M.V. Sridhar, in its meeting on 23 March 2017, the CoA decided to double the fixed component of player compensation. Thus, category A, B and C would receive ₹2 crore, ₹1 crore and ₹50 lakh, respectively, which was double of what they had been receiving. It was also decided to fix match fees at ₹15 lakh for Test matches and at ₹6 lakh and ₹3 lakh for One Day International (ODI) and T20 matches, respectively.

Upon these enhanced remuneration being announced, the media carried a comment by Ravi Shastri, stating that the BCCI pays 'peanuts' to its players.[36] I am in total agreement with him. The richest Board in the world cannot be paying 'peanuts' to its players, the very people who make it the richest body. My only point is: why had everyone stayed silent till then? Why had abundant noise not been made about the fact that forget the conversion of the 'peanuts' to 'almonds', even contracts for the release of these 'peanuts' had not been concluded and the players had not received any remuneration at all that year. It is only when the CoA embarked upon the path of relooking at the entire remuneration structure that voices started to emerge.

There were media reports of players, too, expressing dissatisfaction with the enhanced package. It is true that the enhanced remuneration was still far below what the English and Australian players were receiving.[37] Nevertheless, I assured the

---

[36]Sikdar, Sandip. 'Indian Cricketers' Salary of Rs.2 Crore Is "Peanuts"': Ravi Shastri', 3 April 2017, NDTV Sports, https://bit.ly/3G5sTDS. Accessed on 31 August 2021.

[37]That is still well short (the highest fee of ₹2 crore) of the £700,000 ($870,800) retainers that England's top cricketers, such as Alastair Cook or Joe Root are on, according to media reports, or the A$1.12 million for Australian captain

players that we would consult them and create an appropriate remuneration package comparable to what players abroad were receiving. Additionally, we also ensured that the Team India Test players were adequately compensated so that they did not have to chase IPL contracts.

Following up on this announcement, I had an informal meeting with Virat Kohli and M.S. Dhoni at the ITC Maurya in Delhi on 31 October 2017, to better understand the issues that were agitating the minds of the cricketers. The meeting proved fruitful as the players opened up and were very cooperative in suggesting some remedial measures that needed to be taken. The first issue that came up for discussion was the workload the players were being made to take on. In 2016, they had played for about 232 days and it was taking a heavy toll on them. It emerged that while drawing up the Future Tours Programme (FTP)[38], the players had not been consulted. The IPL fixtures are high-intensity games involving travel between different venues and each team playing a minimum of 14 matches; thus, the gap before and after the IPL games needed to be a minimum of a fortnight.

Another issue discussed in the meeting was the players' contracts and compensation packages. Considering that ours was one of the best teams in the world, the remuneration was lacking when compared with the English or Australian teams. I assured the players that each of these issues would be addressed to their satisfaction. Other issues that came up for discussion included the team's hotel accommodation while travelling abroad, mode of travel, families accompanying players, etc. The meeting

---

Steve Smith. See: 'BCCI Doubles Player Salaries, Hikes Match Fees| Reuters', *Firstpost*, 22 March 2017, https://bit.ly/3f1jocN. Accessed on 31 August 2021.
[38]International cricket matches, played under the aegis of the ICC, are regulated under a comprehensive schedule drawn up in consultation with all the stakeholders and shared with the ICC. The schedule is termed as the Future Tours Programme (FTP).

surely provided me important insight into the issues that needed redressal.

In view of our commitment to consult the players and factor in their suggestions while finalizing the FTP and remuneration package for the next season, the CoA held a formal meeting with team management comprising Ravi Shastri, M.S. Dhoni and Virat Kohli on 30 November in New Delhi. The first issue that came up for discussion was 'player burn out'. Teams are constantly on the move and matches are increasingly scheduled with an eye on generating revenue for the host association rather than the players' fatigue and well-being.[39] This, in my opinion, is inexcusable as players are the very people who make up the riches of the BCCI and causing player burn out is akin to 'killing the goose that lays the golden egg'. This issue was discussed at length and it was decided to provide a fortnight's gap before every foreign tour.

The CEO then explained the FTP for 2019–2023 prepared by Gaurav Saxena, who, being an excellent professional, had taken care of all aspects in preparing the three-year schedule. The discussion was around the number of matches—Tests, T20s and ODIs—that would be played, both at home and away, and the gaps between tournaments. The FTP, as had been proposed, met with the acceptance of the team management. The minutes of the CoA meeting, which are on the BCCI website, record:

> FTP (2019–2023). Mr Rahul Johri presented the proposal for international FTP 2019–23. The team representatives [Kohli, Dhoni and Shastri] appreciated the efforts of the BCCI team in addressing their concerns on the high number of

---

[39]A journalist mentioned to me that in the course of a match being played in Dharamshala in 2016, some players had raised the issue of heavy workload (cramped schedules). They were told by the Board functionaries that if they felt that the schedule was too cramped, they could opt out of the matches as for every vacancy in the team there were 150 persons waiting to fill the slot.

playing days per season, long overseas tours and preparation time before a marquee series/event and gave their consent to the proposed FTP.[40]

The discussion then moved on to the annual player gradation and remuneration structure. The BCCI designates its contracted players into three categories: A, B and C. On this issue, Dhoni came up with an interesting proposition: there should be another category, A+, which should include players who play in all formats of the game. Another very commendable suggestion made by Dhoni and Kohli was that the remuneration package for the more senior and better-known players was not so important, since they earn sufficient amounts from endorsements, and that it is the B and C category players who need to be compensated better as they do not have other sources of income. I really appreciated this spirit of speaking up for their other teammates. In light of this suggestion, we decided on what I describe as a kind of 'pyramid which was flat at the top'. In this structure, the gap between A and B categories would not be very wide and the B and C categories deserved a bigger hike to bring them closer to the remuneration package of the A category.

The discussions were very fruitful and vastly appreciated by the players. The minutes of the meeting record the following:

1. Mr Johri presented a blueprint of the annual player gradation.
2. The team representatives appreciated the efforts of the BCCI team and emphasized on giving importance to the long format of the game and the Test specialist, while finalizing the proposal.
3. Mr Johri invited Mr Santosh Rangnekar (then CFO,

---

[40] Minutes of the meeting of the CoA, 30 November 2017, BCCI, https://cutt.ly/VP5yiox. Accessed on 14 February 2022.

BCCI) to present the methodology used to calculate the gross revenue share (GRS) which leads to the annual retainership fee.
4. (After discussion) *The CoA decided that the proposal should be reconsidered to address the concerns and suggestions made by the team representatives for both international and domestic cricket* (emphasis added to illustrate the fact that the proposal was being redone to incorporate suggestions proposed by the team—this was an entirely new phenomenon, as per their own admission. Never in the past had players been consulted while drawing up the FTP).[41]
5. As per the suggestion of team management, we devised four categories, A+, A, B and C, and the remuneration contemplated was ₹8 crore, ₹7 crore, ₹5 crore and ₹3 crore, respectively.

In our eagerness to ensure that we take the elected office-bearers and the GB of the BCCI along, we referred all the proposed enhancements to the Finance Committee (FC) for their consideration on 12 January 2018. We learnt, to our dismay, that even the decision regarding the ad hoc increase of remuneration, which was decided in a meeting on 22–23 March 2017 was awaiting clearance from the FC.

While the chairman of the committee, Jyotiraditya Scindia, had responded promptly to our request to schedule a meeting on 29 January 2018, the treasurer, who is the convenor of the FC, informed us that there was a court hearing on that day and hence a new date would be intimated. The CoA was forced to decide that the FC had been given sufficient time, and since the matter had been considerably delayed, the CoA would go ahead

---

[41]'Committee of Administrators Approves Pay Hike for Team India', *India Today*, 30 November 2017, https://bit.ly/3q0LX0i. Accessed on 31 August 2021.

and announce the decision.[42] That put paid to all efforts to build consensus. We decided to go ahead and fix the remuneration which was later finally accepted at the SGM held on 22 June 2018.

The fundamental point established by the CoA was that the players, who are the lung, heart and nerve centre of the BCCI, and the fountainhead of the so-called richness of the BCCI, were not being given the due that was truly theirs. It is only because of these players that the BCCI and state associations have become attractive bodies, so much so that the highest in the land want to be its office-bearers. And yet, the disdainful attitude of the office-bearers towards a decision involving the players—the CoA decision of March 2017, enhancing the compensation package—was cleared by the SGM 15 months later!

I have provided a copy of the minutes solely for a peek into how administration was conducted in the institution. It makes for an entertaining reading. The minutes, which were obviously drafted even before the SGM took place, make reference to issues which had no relevance and did not see the light of day, let alone any follow-up activity.

Our focus was not just on taking care of the active players. Much noise has been made of the fate that 'one-time greats' face after they retire from active cricket. There have been horror stories of well-known former cricketers not being able to pay their hospital bills, or living in penury due to no alternative source of income. Pending issues regarding 'one-time benefit' to former women cricketers and monthly gratis amounts were brought to the fore.

Prof. Shetty was familiar with the background. He helped us work out reasonable amounts which former women cricketers deserved, and in the meeting on 22–23 March 2017, a one-

---

[42]Minutes of the meeting of the CoA, 27 February 2018, BCCI, https://cutt.ly/7P5yhuv. Accessed on 14 February 2022.

time benefit of amounts ranging from ₹15 lakh to ₹30 lakh, was approved. Monthly gratis of ₹15,000 to ₹22,500 per month was also approved. The amount payable was based on the number of matches the former cricketer had played. A corresponding change was made to amounts payable to male cricketers to bring them to par.

As I write, I am reminded of an observation made by Qaiser Mohammad Ali, a senior journalist for *Outlook*, who wrote: 'Any event in Indian cricket, however routine, always has all the makings of a nail-biting game. It comes with a dose of drama, mystery, innuendo, allegations by anonymous people...'[43] This decision too had its share of 'oversight' by the office-bearers. The then treasurer wrote to the CEO:

> I am sure whispers would have reached your ears as well, but there is a lot of buzz regarding Ms Diana Edulji ji and some decisions and connotations are being drawn with regard to conflict of interest. Whether it is the one-time benefit to women cricketers where she and her sister are beneficiaries, or it is the enhancement of the gratis amount or the additional women players added to the gratis list or it is addition to the men cricketers in the 1–9 category for OTB, some of whom are supposedly her colleagues in the Mumbai cricket association... I would also like to draw your attention to the fact that though Mr N Srinivasan had recused himself from the meetings of the IPL on the issue relating to CSK when he had a stake in it, the Hon'ble court did hold some of those as instances of conflict of interest... I could have waited to be bypassed as Diana ji has suggested in her e mail and then raised this issue once it was done as she has not only been vocal about these

---

[43] Ali, Qaiser Mohammad. 'Neither One to Blink First', *Outlook*, 12 June 2017, https://cutt.ly/oP5ynRz. Accessed on 14 February 2022.

payments but has been feverishly following it up with the treasury department...

Fortunately, on both the dates that this issue was discussed by the CoA, Diana had recused herself from the discussions and it was Prof. Shetty who guided us. It certainly would not have been fair to ask or expect Diana and/or her sister, to refuse the one-time benefit payment that was being made to all other retired women cricketers just because she was a member of the CoA.

'C' WORD MUDDIES THE PITCH

The BCCI's long innings in the courts started with issues regarding conflict of interest. It was thus imperative that the Lodha Committee concentrate on this aspect while recommending a constitutional framework. However, a straitjacketed application of the proscriptions proved to be counter-effective and disproportionately restrictive on current and former players. It is commonly accepted that any contract or arrangement that defeats the objective of fair play or objectivity, especially when it deals with commercial interest, will be repugnant to public policy.

So, while the BCCI mandates these norms for its full-time employees, it cannot be made applicable to all Indian cricketers, coaches, team support professionals and commentators, and the like merely because they are associated with the game of cricket. For example, if a person is employed as a full-time coach by the BCCI, he should not undertake any other assignment from an IPL franchise or a media company. On the other hand, if a retired cricketer is doing commentary for a private channel, it would be grossly unfair to stop him from being a coach or mentor to an IPL team. This norm becomes all the more unfair when it is applied only to Indian professionals as it gives an underhand advantage to foreigners plying their skills in India. Thus, a Ricky Ponting could be the coach of an IPL team while in another role in an Australian entity such that after the expiry of his engagement with the Indian franchise, he is allowed to return to Australia and ply his trade there, whilst an Indian commentator is not permitted to be the coach of any IPL team.

Conflicts have been classified as tractable and intractable. Instances where someone runs a players' academy and is appointed a selector or when a relative of an office-bearer is granted a catering contract, are intractable conflicts that cannot be resolved by recusal and require dismissal or divestment. The tractable ones are resolvable and excusable through recusal with full disclosure. Unfortunately, the norms laid down in the new constitution did not permit the CoA the freedom of making a distinction.

It was such straitjacketed norms built into the Lodha reform that instigated a complaint of conflict of interest against stalwarts such as Sachin Tendulkar, Sourav Ganguly and V.V.S Laxman, who were doing yeoman service in the Cricket Advisory Committee (CAC), on a purely pro bono basis. The ethics officer took this complaint on record. He could also interpret the rule only by the letter of the law as accepted by the Supreme Court. He issued a notice to the CAC members. The CoA was called to give its comments on the issue and it could do so as per the same rule.

We informed the ethics officer of the tractability of such a conflict which could be remedied by full disclosure. In any case, the engagement of the CAC members was totally part-time. Their services were being availed only once in two or three years. No distinguished cricketer of the standing of the CAC members at that time would accept to guide the BCCI if they were precluded from taking up any other assignment with any other private agency just because they were CAC members on a pro bono basis with the BCCI.

Absolute prohibition on former players from occupying multiple posts is unduly restrictive. I am of the opinion that former international players who possess outstanding cricketing skills and who are not under long-term contract with the BCCI or its administration, should be allowed to hold multiple posts so long as the performance of duties associated with the occupation of each post is not compromised by holding such simultaneous posts. It is only in the long-term interest of Indian cricket to ensure that posts which require individuals with cricketing skills and experience are treated differently or else these cricketing icons who are engaged elsewhere will not be able to lend their expertise to Indian cricketers.

Being convinced of the rigidity and unfairness of such a rule, the CoA, in its eleventh and last status report, recommended to the Court that the ethics officer should be permitted the flexibility in determination of conflict of interest. The CoA also recommended that it is unreasonable to prohibit active players, who do not have central contracts with the BCCI, from holding posts simultaneously, especially, those that do not compromise or prejudice the performance of duties with an adverse impact on the larger interests of the game. It should also be mandated that every individual make full disclosure of any existing or potential action that may cause a conflict before the engagement or contract. This disclosure should be put in the public domain. On the other hand, a former player who is not under contract with the BCCI may be permitted to engage with the CAC or assist a franchisee or broadcaster after making the required disclosure. This will help the BCCI in better utilizing the cricketing expertise of distinguished players of the game as also provide them adequate avenues for a career beyond their active cricketing years.

Cricket is the pride of our country, and the BCCI is the face of Indian cricket. It has to be administered in a manner in which each player takes pride in being a part of the BCCI and gives his best. The player should not be beset with scandals and allegations that surround his parent body or have any odium against its elected administrators. Its management and administrative practices should reflect best governance principles. Any well-wisher of Indian cricket and its administration should abide by the principles of transparency, accountability and professional management by a credibly elected body. Sports administrators, particularly in a democratically elected body, have a social responsibility. There is a principle of separation of elected chairman and CEO roles, which need to be scrupulously followed. There can be no two views on this. It is only when the administration of the BCCI is premised on an edifice of probity and accountability that the institution can seek the same from players and the support staff.

The CoA realized that administration is not a walk in the park. It is also not about having an opinion and insisting on its acceptance irrespective of circumstances and others' viewpoints. It involves a 360-degree examination of all aspects, weighing every opinion, building consensus and then deciding the course of action. Each issue needs to be addressed and resolved at an appropriate time. It was very necessary for all four of us to see through the same lens and function as a team. Since all of us had played a good amount of cricket and had been members of a team in our earlier days, this was possible.

Teamwork held us in good stead when we embarked on our second immediate task—to salvage and make the best of a bad situation that had been served to us in the BCCI vs ICC revenue and governance model. It required understanding the 'interest groups', following their tentacles, looking for an apt time to clip them and dealing with each 'interested party' on its own terms.

Were the ghostbusters ready for this chin music? Only time would tell.

3

DELIVERING ON THE GOVERNANCE AND REVENUE MODEL

The summer of 2017 brought with it more than its fair share of blistering heat. Publications across the country added to the rising temperatures with headlines that were scathing and unforgiving: 'Indian Cricket Board Loses Governance, Revenue Votes at ICC Meet in Dubai'[44], 'Red-Faced BCCI Loses Vote on Revenue and ICC Constitution Revamp'[45], 'BCCI Loses Big Time as ICC Votes for New Revenue-Share Model'[46]. As if these were not enough, another one read: 'SC-Appointed CoA Needs to Be Sacked for Failure to Protect Indian Cricket's Clout and Revenue'[47].

---

[44]Patra, Sajal Kumar. 'Indian Cricket Board Loses Governance, Revenue Votes at ICC Meet in Dubai', NDTV, 26 April 2017, https://bit.ly/3GfN9Ts. Accessed on 14 February 2022.

[45]Ali, Qaiser Mohammad. 'Red-Faced BCCI Loses Vote on Revenue and ICC Constitution Revamp', *Outlook,* 27 April 2017, https://cutt.ly/aP5yID2. Accessed on 14 February 2022.

[46]'BCCI Loses Big Time as ICC Votes for New Revenue-Share Model', *The Economic Times*, 27 April 2017, https://bit.ly/334Jdqb. Accessed on 14 February 2022.

[47]Jagannathan, R. 'SC-Appointed CoA Needs to Be Sacked for Failure to Protect Indian Cricket's Clout and Revenue', *Swarajya*, 28 April 2017, https://bit.ly/3f7hFml. Accessed on 14 February 2022.

The CoA was the whipping boy!

These were the general reactions of the well-informed, the not so well-informed and those whose interest was best served by the misinformation. The factual position, as is quite usual, was very different. However, in all fairness to the above-mentioned headlines, the BCCI, had indeed, lost its financial clout in the ICC. However, this clout, which it had claimed to have gained, more by brawn than brain, was ill-fated and met a quick demise. The backlash that the BCCI faced in 2016 was the consequence of a rather crude, ill-advised and ill-thought-out attempt to snatch a larger share of the ICC revenue pie. To understand why the BCCI had landed in this most unfortunate position, where it not only lost clout but also a tremendous amount of goodwill, we need to put the entire issue in a proper perspective, particularly through the lens of independent cricket watchers.

DIFFERING STANCES ON REFORM

About a decade ago, the ICC decided to adopt reform measures and took steps in that direction. In October 2011, the ICC commissioned an independent governance review committee headed by Lord Woolf (the Rt. Hon. Lord Woolf of Barnes), a former Chief Justice of England and Wales.[48] The report, presented in February 2012, suggested sweeping reforms in the administration of cricket and the functioning of the governing body of the ICC. The report sought to restructure the ICC governing board and make it more independent and less dominated by the 'big' cricket-playing nations. It proposed a revisit of the rights and benefits of the Full Member Test-playing nations. It recommended

---

[48]Lord Woolf and PricewaterhouseCoopers LLP. *An Independent Governance Review of the International Cricket Council,* PricewaterhouseCoopers LLP, 1 February 2012, https://cutt.ly/QP5yHmp. Accessed on 14 February 2022.

greater equity, transparency and inclusiveness among the ICC and its members.

Addressing the imbalance among the cricket-playing nations, it sought the revamping of the Executive Board by inducting independent directors (five) in keeping with best corporate practices, convert the membership tiers to two from the then three, do away with the affiliate category and reduce the numerical strength of the Full Members. The report also recommended that an ICC director should not concurrently hold any leadership or executive post with their home boards. For example, at that time, the BCCI president was a director of the ICC, but in compliance with this recommendation, he would have to give up presidentship of the home board if he desired to continue in the ICC. It also suggested that 'non-Test-playing' countries should get more opportunities to compete against the top nations and argued for an increased say for them in the administration of the game.

Another major recommendation of the Woolf report[49] was that the current number of Full Members[50] should be reconsidered. The report maintained that Test status should not be the criterion for full membership and that even 'other high-performing (but not test-playing) members' should be included. (A Full Member gets greater access to the ICC's funds and greater voting power in the governing body's chief executive committee among others.) The report noted that the ICC had reached a stage where if cricket had to be a truly international game, it must act in the best interests of cricket generally, and promote, lead and develop the international game.

As is the fate of most such recommendations seeking reform, change or transformation, the Woolf report too got placed aside

---

[49]Incidentally, Lord Woolf's advisor on the review, particularly in relation to the cricket scene in India, was the former Chief Justice of the Punjab and Haryana High Court, Justice Mukul Mudgal.
[50]In the ICC parlance, Full Members were Test-playing nations.

to adorn a shelf in the ICC. In 2014, the ICC did a complete volte-face, and in the garb of adopting a more market-led structure, proposed a diametrically opposite concept which gave prominence to the 'Big Three' model. The Big Three identified in terms of key revenue and profit drivers in the ICC were the ECB, CA and the BCCI. They were given stewardship roles by allotting them key functions in all the core committees. The proposal for revamp was drafted by a working group of the ICC's Finance and Commercial Affairs Committee, which obviously had the Big Three as members. It is believed that the BCCI, with N. Srinivasan as its president[51], had played a lead role in this revamp proposal.

This proposal recommended very broad amendments to the administrative structure, the FTP and the revenue devolution pattern. It involved the setting up of a new Executive Committee in which the Big Three would have permanent membership; this committee would have the power to override all other committees. It would become 'the sole recommendation committee...on all constitutional, personnel, integrity, ethics, development and nominations affairs.'[52] A rotational post of an independent chairman with a two-year tenure was conceptualized. This would considerably encroach on the powers of the president in the then existing model. The key positions of ICC chairman and chairpersons of the main committees such as finance and commercial affairs would have to be nominees of the Big Three. This model gave the Big Three total

---

[51]In September 2011, N. Srinivasan had taken over as president of the BCCI from Shashank Manohar. However, in June 2013, Jagmohan Dalmiya was appointed interim president after Srinivasan had to step aside till a probe into his son-in-law's alleged involvement in spot-fixing in 2013 was completed. Srinivasan became president again in October 2013. On 2 March 2015, Dalmiya again replaced Srinivasan.
[52]Ugra, Sharda. 'Big Three Could Control Revamped ICC', *ESPN cricinfo*, 18 January 2014, https://es.pn/3G7RCr4. Accessed on 31 August 2021.

control over administrative and cricketing matters and a sizeable chunk of the revenues, ostensibly on the argument that they were the principal revenue earners for the ICC.

The proposal focused attention on the extant revenue distribution pattern of the ICC, terming it as 'distorted', since it did not factor in the contribution of the individual members to the revenue pool. The extant devolution formula distributed surplus revenues equally among the Full Members and in smaller proportions to the Associate and Affiliate Members. The underlying principle was that 75 per cent of the ICC's surplus revenue will be allocated equitably among its 10 Full Members or in other words, 7.5 per cent to each Full Member. The 'distortion' was that Full Members such as Zimbabwe were treated as equal to others like the BCCI, ECB or CA, though their contribution to revenue was negligible.

As a consequence, there was no incentive for a Full Member to increase its contribution to the revenue as it would continue to receive the same proportion, regardless of its contribution. The model also did not account for the opportunity cost borne by any of the Big Three for participating in ICC events. That means, if these Full Members held home-series events during the time that they otherwise spend in participating in ICC events, then they would earn significantly more and this opportunity was being foregone in order to participate in ICC events.

A proposal to introduce the concept of 'contribution cost' based on contribution to revenue and opportunity cost for participating in ICC events was made. This contribution cost, expressed as a percentage of the revenue, was to be treated as cost and deducted from the total revenue to arrive at the surplus. It was only from this surplus that Full Members would get 7.5 per cent as before. This was to be in addition to the 'contribution cost' earlier paid out as cost. The model allocated 32 per cent as 'contribution cost', out of which 20.3 per cent was determined as the BCCI's share. Assuming revenue to be $2.5 billion for the cycle 2015–2023, it was expected that the BCCI would be receiving $507 million as its 'contribution cost' plus another $62 million as its share of the surplus, taking the total to $569 million. Hence, the magic figure of $570 million that was being projected as revenue receivable by the BCCI under the Big Three formula.

No sooner had these new set of proposals been placed before the ICC member nations (on 9 January 2014), that murmurs broke out among members labelling it as a retrograde step. A letter addressed to Alan Isaac (then ICC president) and signed among others by Malcolm Speed (former CEO of the ICC), Malcolm Gray (former chairman of the Australian Cricket Board and former ICC CEO), Clive Lloyd, Ali Bacher (then United Cricket Board of South Africa managing director) and Ehsan Mani (former chairman, Pakistan Cricket Board) expressed disappointment. They claimed that the proposal lacked vision and the ICC needed a less parochial approach. They drew attention to the animosity that had existed prior to 1993, when England and Australia had veto rights.[53]

Commenting on the ICC's potential revamp proposal, former England Test cricketer Sir Geoffrey (Geoff) Boycott felt that the two-tier Test system will sound the death knell for certain teams. He went on to say, 'I am appalled by [the] pure greed of the Big Three.'[54]

Reflecting the views of most of the member countries, *The Guardian* summarized it as:

---

[53] ANI. 'Former Oz, Pak, South Africa Cricket Chiefs Oppose ICC "Big Three" Revamp Move', *Business Standard*, 27 January 2014, https://bit.ly/3FbaW5q. Accessed on 18 October 2021.

[54] 'Appalled by Pure Greed of the Big Three', *ESPN cricinfo*, 29 January 2014, https://es.pn/32Wc9AJ. Accessed on 18 October 2021.

> [Then,] through a mixture of chutzpah, cajoling and bullying, the Big Three cricketing nations—Australia, England and India—awarded themselves greater powers, and more ICC cash than the other 102 members combined. One representative of another Test nation felt 'sick' voting through the changes, with persistent fears that India would retaliate against those voting against its wishes by disrupting the cricket calendar.[55]

The ICC, however, proceeded to pursue issues as decided in the proposal and relayed its intent through a press release on 8 February 2014, the relevant extract of which is as follows:

> The ICC Board will continue to be the primary decision-making body. From the start of July this year, the ICC Chairman will be N. Srinivasan from the BCCI... A set of proposals was initially developed by the respective chairs of BCCI, CA and ECB—N. Srinivasan, Wally Edwards and Giles Clarke before being presented to a meeting of the Full Members on 9 January.[56]

A CHANGE OF GUARD

N. Srinivasan, the then president of the BCCI, took over as the first independent chairman of the ICC on 26 June 2014. However, due to a few complaints on which the Supreme Court of India was adjudicating, the BCCI decided, in its 86th AGM, to recall him and nominate its newly elected president, Shashank Manohar,

---

[55] Wigmore, Tim. 'Can Cricket Be Saved from Itself? How the ICC Is Flirting with Essential Reform', *The Guardian,* 16 February 2017, https://bit.ly/3JZgvYf. Accessed on 31 August 2021.
[56] 'Big 3 Get Their Way—ICC Board Approves Changes to Governance, Competition and Financial Models', *sportskeeda*, 8 February 2014, https://bit.ly/33nU5PS. Accessed 1 September 2022.

as the chairman of the world body. Srinivasan demitted office in the ICC on 9 November 2015. Manohar was to replace him for the balance seven months of his two-year tenure. By this time, the BCCI had not received any revenue from the ICC as per the Big Three model described above. It is therefore fair to deduce that the so-called 2014 model, or Big Three model, was never implemented.

Manohar waged a war against conflict of interest and such other issues which were a blemish on the image of the BCCI. Even before he formally took over as the ICC chairman, he announced his desire to reverse the Big Three formula with the objective of introducing equity, transparency and good governance. He announced that he was committed to implementing a wide-ranging reform by introducing decentralization of decision-making and was opposed to the Big Three revenue-sharing formula. Manohar told *The Hindu*:

> I don't agree with the three major countries bullying the ICC… I don't agree with the revenue-sharing formula, because it's nice to say that India (BCCI) will get 22 per cent of the total revenue of the ICC, but you cannot make the poor poorer and the rich richer, only because you have the clout. The ICC runs cricket throughout the world… You should have the best man, whether he comes from Zimbabwe, or West Indies, or even from an associate or affiliate to work on a committee, who will promote the interests of the ICC.[57]

After Manohar took over in November 2015, he found that the majority of the Full Members were against the 2014 formula and wanted it revoked. He was cognizant of the letter written by,

---

[57]Vishwanath, G. 'Major Countries Should Not Bully the ICC', *The Hindu*, 26 November 2015, https://bit.ly/3qXf2ZU. Accessed on 1 September 2021.

inter alia, the managing director of Cricket South Africa seeking a rethink since there was a huge disparity in the payments to the Full Members. Even the chairman of CA had expressed his reservations about the decisions taken at the insistence of the Big Three.[58]

ICC members also informed him that majority of the Full Members felt that they had been forced to agree to the changes in the governance and finance structure because the BCCI had introduced a clause to that effect in the memorandum of understanding (MoU) to be signed with the Full Member Boards, before agreeing to the FTP for the next eight years. He was all the more convinced that the formula based on the 'Big Three' principle was iniquitous and not in the long-term interest of the game. Manohar and his team set about working on the revamp. The Executive Board meeting, held in February 2016, unanimously approved the roll back of the changes made in the governance structure in 2014. The word 'unanimously' would imply that the BCCI representative was also agreeable to this.

This decision of the Executive Board caused concern to all the supporters of the 2014 formula in the BCCI. It was decided that the GB should discuss the issues involved, and a SGM was convened on 19 February 2016. For better appreciation of the situation and for the reader to get the correct perspective, I reproduce below the requisite extract of the minutes of the SGM which was held a full year ahead of the ICC passing the resolution in principle, in February 2017:[59]

> Item No. 2: To Discuss and Decide on the Financial Structure of the Member Boards of the ICC.

---

[58] ANI. 'Former Oz, Pak, South Africa Cricket Chiefs Oppose ICC "Big Three" Revamp Move', *Business Standard*, 27 January 2014, https://bit.ly/3FbaW5q. Accessed on 18 October 2021.
[59] I have quoted the exact wording of the minutes as in BCCI records.

The Chairman[60] informed the members that he had received a letter from the Hon. Secretary TNCA which has been marked to all the affiliated units as well.

The letter seeks clarification on whether as Chairman of ICC, I had agreed to changes in the Governance Structure and in the Financial Structure for distribution of ICC funds between Full Members was approved by the working committee of the Board.

The Chairman informed the members that the ICC Governance Committee and the ICC Executive Board had approved unanimously to change some of the decisions with respect to Governance Structure passed in 2014.

As far as change in the Financial Structure adopted in 2014 was concerned, majority of the Full Members of the ICC were against the same and wanted the same revoked.

The chairman further informed the members that as per the ICC constitution, seven Full Members can get together and reverse any of the earlier decisions taken by the Executive Board. He further pointed out that even the current chairman of Cricket Australia had reservations about the decisions taken at the instance of the Big Three—Cricket Australia, BCCI and ECB.

The chairman pointed out that majority of the Full Members felt that they were forced to agree to the changes in Governance and Financial Structure because the BCCI had a clause introduced to that effect in the MOU to be signed with the Full Member Boards before agreeing to the FTP for the next eight years.

He informed the House, [that the] Executive Board held in February 2016 unanimously agreed to the rollback

---

[60]Shashank Manohar was still president of the BCCI then and chair of this SGM. Anurag Thakur was the secretary.

of the changes made in the Governance Structure in 2014.

The Chairman also pointed out that at the last meeting of the ICC Executive Board, he had assured the Full Members that he would discuss the matter on Financial Structure internally with the BCCI Working Committee and make a proposal at the next meeting to be held in April 2016.

The Chairman then invited members to give their views on the matter.

Mr Anirudh Chaudhury stated that he was against any changes in the Financial Structure implemented in 2014 which was approved by the Working Committee. He felt that all the Full members of the ICC had agreed to the financial structure with full knowledge and now they cannot go back on the same.

He further stated that no documents had been placed at this meeting so any proposal for a change in the finance structure approved by ICC in 2014 would not be proper.

Mr Sharad Pawar opined that while it is correct that BCCI should get a share of the money based on the fact that 70% of the media rights revenue comes from India, we must also remember that Pakistan Board, Sri Lanka Board, Bangladesh Board, Zimbabwe Cricket, South Africa had always supported India in good and bad times. A revision of the Financial Structure by which the BCCI gets a major share and the other Boards also get enough to help them to develop and promote cricket should be welcome. It was important for BCCI to ensure the level of cricket grows in all the member countries for the future of this game and BCCI should take care of the member Boards who have always stood by it.

Mr P.S. Raman felt that chairman could be authorized to find a solution which does not largely compromise the formula which BCCI worked out in 2014.

Mr Brijesh Patel and Mr Niranjan Shah supported the views of Mr P.S. Raman.

The House except Mr Anirudh Chaudhury agreed with this proposal and it was resolved as under:

> It is hereby resolved that the Hon. President and the Hon. Secretary be authorized to negotiate the Financial structure approved in 2014 keeping in mind the larger interest of the BCCI.

They would report the same to the Working Group of the Board.

It is further resolved that the Hon. President and Hon. Secretary are authorized to renegotiate the FTP for the next eight-year cycle.

The chairman thanked the members for the faith reposed in him and he assured the House that he would ensure that the renegotiated financial terms would form a part of the Rules and Regulations of the ICC.

As can be seen from the trend of discussions in the SGM, the BCCI was only focused on the revenue-sharing model. The SGM, after detailed deliberation, finally passed resolutions only to 'negotiate the financial structure approved in 2014 keeping in mind the larger interest of the BCCI and renegotiate the FTP for the next eight year-cycle'. There was *no mention* of the governance model.

It is of significance that the change in the stance of the BCCI took place in the aforementioned SGM wherein everyone left it to the president and secretary to negotiate the 2014 model. The Big Three formula, which had been thrust on the ICC in 2014, found no backing in the BCCI. The Executive Board of the ICC, under the chairmanship of Manohar, decided to roll back that formula in February 2016, and here was the SGM of the BCCI convened in February 2016, a full year before the CoA took over, seeking to also resile from it.

The CoA inherited *that* decision, when it came into existence on 30 January 2017. In the same month, the ICC introduced various proposals for consideration in the February meeting, for carrying out changes to the constitution regarding the Memorandum and Articles of Association as well as the basis on which the ICC distributes funds to its members. The ICC meetings were scheduled from 2 to 5 February 2017. The Court directed the BCCI to be represented by Amitabh Choudhary, the honorary joint secretary, who had been permitted by the Court to officiate as the secretary[61], Anirudh Chaudhry, the honorary treasurer, and Vikram Limaye, the CoA member.

ICC'S HOSTILE WELCOME

We need to perceive the situation that the CoA was confronted with. Within two days of its taking over, the CoA had to learn the nuances of the 2014 model of governance and how the 2017 decision would lead to resiling from it. On one side were a select few, loyal to the 2014 model, who had sold the dream of the BCCI getting $570 million as their revenue share from the ICC. Their story had been dashed in the decision of the February 2016 meeting of the ICC Executive Board. On the other side was the revamped model which had been approved, in principle, by the Executive Board, chaired by Manohar, and had been circulated for consideration in the February 2017 meeting of the ICC. This formula had been explained by Manohar, as BCCI president, in the SGM meeting on 19 February 2016. As per this formula, the

---

[61]Since Ajay Shirke, the honorary secretary, had been removed by the order of 2 January 2017.

BCCI was to receive $290 million. The BCCI president, who had chaired the SGM in February 2016, was now introducing the new formula in the ICC in his new avatar as chairman. He had thanked the SGM members for the faith reposed in him and also assured that the renegotiated financial terms would form a part of the rules of the ICC.

After all, this had been discussed and decided. What other stand could the CoA take? However, what was played up in public domain was the fact that the inexperienced CoA did not have a clue about how to handle the situation and that experienced cricket administrators would have been able to use the BCCI's clout effectively to regain lost ground.

Sadly, what was not played up was that within the two days that the CoA got to prepare its position, Limaye literally worked 24/7 to devise an alternative formula which was a win–win for all members. It would have provided the BCCI higher revenue without comprising on the principles of equity and transparency. A couple of members of the ICC, whom we consulted, were willing to go along with this alternative too, but there was no time to consult all the member nations.

In the February meeting of the ICC, we sought more time to consider and respond to the proposals but majority of the members were far too committed to the revamp. The ICC proceeded to pass a resolution agreeing in principle to accept the proposals, subject to further views that may be expressed before finalizing the same at the next meeting to be held in April.

Readers would recall that many ICC members have revealed that they were forced into accepting the Big Three formula. I have also maintained that it was more brawn than brain that had been deployed to gain consent. The same pattern is witnessed when we fast forward to the February 2017 meeting. *The Guardian* commented:

In Dubai, one Board of Control for Cricket in India representative's response was to revert to the organisation's notorious tactics of yore—threatening to pull out of ICC events and tours and lengthening the Indian Premier League, in between promising extra matches as sweeteners to those who sided with India… Anirudh Chaudhry, one of the BCCI's representatives in Dubai, was said to be deeply uncooperative. Chaudhry, a known ally of the governing body's former chairman, suggested India's support for the new cricket structures depended on them being happy with any finance and governance reforms, and made various threats…

And hence the final conclusion by *The Guardian*: 'The [ICC] board knew about this, was very unimpressed and this led to a real resolve among the members not to be bullied again'.[62]

What else does one conclude from these independent references? Only that what was ham-handedly attempted to be thrust upon other cricketing nations had to boomerang, and boomerang it sure did!

The die had been cast. Anything that the CoA tried to do after that was not destined to produce any favourable result. The CoA went about trying to salvage what had been allowed to dissipate over a one-year period. The CoA opened the lines of communication with the ICC chairman and other important members. The attempt was to negotiate a higher share of the revenues from the $290 million that was on offer. In the 26 April meeting of the ICC, the BCCI's share continued to be $290 million with the BCCI getting only two votes in their favour and eight against (Sri Lanka voted with us).

---

[62] Wigmore, Tim. 'Can Cricket Be Saved from Itself? How the ICC Is Flirting with Essential Reform' *The Guardian*, 16 February 2017, https://bit.ly/3qWxi5u. Accessed on 6 September 2021.

Unfortunately, the BCCI had got so obsessed with trying to protect personal interests, such as seeking the Supreme Court to review its orders on disqualification for those over 70 years of age, withdrawal of the cooling-off clause and disqualification after completing nine years as an office-bearer in state associations/BCCI, that issues of governance and financial models with the ICC appeared to have got second priority.

MAKING THE CUT

Not having learnt a lesson from the drubbing that we got in the February meetings of the ICC, we continued to display brawn where brain was required. The ICC Champions Trophy was scheduled to be held in the United Kingdom (UK) in June, and 25 April was the deadline for all participants to name their squad. India had not named its squad as yet. The refrain that was gathering momentum was that we should withdraw from the Champions Trophy. The media was constantly playing up the loss: 'Snubbed by ICC, BCCI Threatens to Withdraw from Champions Trophy 2017'.[63]

Even though cricketing icons such as Sachin Tendulkar and Rahul Dravid were unanimous in wanting the team to play in the tournament[64], the CoA was being pressurized by all and sundry in the 'old guard' to withdraw the team. The argument was that India withdrawing would render the tournament a financial failure.

Withdrawing from the tournament was not an easy decision to take, least of all by a court-appointed body as compared with

---

[63] Devendra Pandey and Shamik Chakrabarty. 'Snubbed by ICC, BCCI Threatens to Withdraw from Champions Trophy 2017', *The Indian Express*, 7 September 2016, https://bit.ly/3AeYktf. Accessed on 20 January 2022.
[64] "Sachin Tendulkar, Rahul Dravid Want Indian Cricket Team to Play Champions Trophy', *Hindustan Times*, 4 May 2017, https://bit.ly/3q9xlf6. Accessed on 18 October 2021.

an elected body. Our team had prepared over two years for the tournament. We had just about the best team in the world at that time. This was all besides the fact that the withdrawal would create a huge legal and financial mess. More importantly, the Indian cricket-loving population was eagerly awaiting the cricketing carnival. They would fault the BCCI for throwing away India's chances of winning the trophy, and rightly so, to pursue its personal battles under the delusion that the mirage of $570 million was actually receivable. As it was, the image of the BCCI had taken a huge beating in the public's perception what with match-fixing, conflict of interest and multiple inquiry reports creating avoidable opprobrium around its functioning.

The pressure on the CoA was to send a legal notice to the ICC of our right to withdraw the team from participating in the tournament, even if we did not really carry out the threat later. The advice was that it would at least jolt the ICC. This really was living in wonderland. Issue a notice to a person (the chairman of ICC) who had been a former president of the BCCI? A person who had participated in the SGM of 19 February 2016 and was well acquainted with the decision of the SGM, and yet, our 'experienced pundits' felt that he would buckle to their 'brinkmanship', specially when he had 13 votes in his favour against the BCCI's solitary vote! All this chest beating was totally unwarranted. The ICC chair had kept the doors open and had assured our representatives, in the February meeting, that he would look at the proposal favourably.

Taking all these aspects into consideration, the CoA requested the members to hold an SGM and decide on the stance that the BCCI should take. The SGM was scheduled for 7 May 2017.

Soon, the CoA realized that, despite the decision taken in the February 2016 SGM, there was an ill-advised campaign to persuade BCCI's member associations to sign a resolution for the issuance of a legal notice to the ICC. On 2 May, the media reported that the honorary treasurer of the BCCI, Anirudh Chaudhry, had circulated a letter to the member states to muster opinion for boycotting the Champions Trophy and, as an initial attempt, issue a legal notice to the ICC:

> BCCI treasurer Anirudh Chaudhry has asked full members of the board to issue a letter to Amitabh Chaudhry stating that the Indian board has approved the decision to send a notice to the IBC/ICC to cure the breach as per the terms of the Members Participation Agreement immediately...
>
> However, the BCCI has been in no mood to relent. A faction in the Indian board is keen on threatening the ICC with a boycott of the ICC Champions Trophy to be held in England next month.
>
> But the Committee of Administrators is against any such move and wants unanimity on the issue. Anirudh, through his letter, is seeking to get a clear majority in a bid to issue the Champions Trophy boycott threat.[65]

What was disconcerting about these insidious attempts was that the news item mentioned 'that the Indian board has approved the decision to send a notice to the IBC/ICC'. No such decision had been taken. To ensure that the ongoing dialogue that the acting secretary and the CEO were having with the ICC chairman under the guidance of the CoA does not get disrupted, we were compelled to issue directions to the effect that:

> All letters, notices and other correspondence on behalf of the BCCI which seek to invoke or exercise any rights/remedies under the Members Participation Agreement entered into between the BCCI and the ICC Business Corporation FZ-

---

[65]'BCCI Treasurer Anirudh Chaudhary Tries to Create Unanimity Among Members on Champions Trophy Boycott Threat', *India Today*, 2 May 2017, https://bit.ly/3tHj5MU. Accessed on 20 January 2022.

LLC ('IBC') shall only be issued with the prior approval of the Committee of Administrators.[66]

It was clarified that the direction would apply to all matters of communication which purport to invoke any of our rights or remedies before the ICC.

Considering all the misinformation that was floating around, the CoA convened two sets of meetings with the different member associations to clarify to them the discussions with the ICC that were taking place. Member associations appeared to be of a more mature opinion and did not favour any confrontationist stand. These meetings were held before the SGM scheduled for 7 May to discuss this and some other issues. However, since this was a legacy issue that the CoA had inherited, we wrote to the acting secretary prior to the SGM that the uncertainty sought to be created was adversely impacting the morale of the players. Inter alia, the letter stated:

> Our discussions with the ICC and other cricket boards have revealed a trust deficit that the BCCI needs to do its part to address… The General Body of the BCCI has itself recognized the need to adopt a collaborative/non-confrontational approach with the ICC and other cricket boards during the Special General Meeting held on 19th February 2016.

The SGM took place on the appointed date. The member state associations unanimously decided to have the Indian team participate in the Champions Trophy, and not send any legal notice or any such confrontational letter to the ICC. The press release after the SGM stated the following: 'The BCCI SGM unanimously decided that the Indian cricket team will participate in the upcoming ICC

---

[66] Viswanath, G. 'Panel Says BCCI Needs Its Permission to Talk to ICC', *The Hindu*, 2 May 2017, https://bit.ly/3C0whhW, accessed on 1 March 2022.

Champions Trophy. The All-India Senior Selection Meeting will be held tomorrow, May 8, in New Delhi to pick the team.'[67]

The unanimous decision on the two issues mentioned above was not without the usual drama that decision-making in the BCCI has come to be associated with. Members who attended the meeting informed us that they were taken by surprise to find that N. Srinivasan had joined the deliberations from London via Skype. Srinivasan began with the proposal to issue a notice to the ICC, but found no support and was cornered, after which the decision to participate was unanimous.[68]

There were other reports also such as: 'It was a setback for the ousted N. Srinivasan faction which was keen to take an aggressive stand. Srinivasan, in fact, joined the discussions via Skype to air his views but didn't take a confrontational stand.'[69] However, there were sane and mature voices like that of the chairman of the IPL GC, Rajeev Shukla. He steered the discussion towards a positive approach—a mature and constructive voice in the entire imbroglio.

That decision drew the curtains on this controversy which had been insidiously created for satisfaction of personal egos. Fortunately, the member associations had begun to think of the larger interest of the game and were not misled into the narrow politics of personalities. They had recognized that if India were to withdraw from the Champions Trophy, it would have led to the BCCI's marginalization from ICC events. Also, that the

---

[67]Boria Majumdar and Ateet Sharma. 'BCCI Authorises Amitabh Choudhury to Defend India's Interests at ICC', *India Today*, 7 May 2017, https://bit.ly/3Ksu6rl. Accessed on 20 January 2022.
[68]'BCCI Clears India's Participation at ICC Champions Trophy', *India Today*, 7 May 2017, https://bit.ly/3FNV6xU. Accessed on 20 January 2022.
[69]PTI. 'BCCI Clears India's. CT Participation, No Legal Notice to ICC', *Deccan Chronicle*, 7 May 2017, https://bit.ly/3tJzvVc. Accessed on 20 January 2022.

adverse fallout of our IPL tournament would have been huge thereby marginalizing Indian cricket further from the mainstream cricketing countries.

Luckily, with the hindsight of the miserable fallout of the arm-twisting that the BCCI had tried to do in 2014, the CoA held its nerves and decided not to withdraw from the tournament. The squad for the Champions Trophy was announced on 8 May. All the office-bearers who had opposed participation flew to the UK to witness the matches.

SWEETEST VICTORY AFTER THE HARDEST BATTLE

This decision helped us negotiate better terms and an enhanced share from the ICC in its final meeting of the board on 23 June 2017. In this final meeting, after repeated rounds of discussion with the ICC chairman, and with his active cooperation, the CoA could ensure that the BCCI's share was fixed at $405 million. This was $115 million more than the earlier decision. At this level, India would receive 22.8 per cent of the ICC's pool. Next on the list was England with $139 million, which was only 7.8 per cent of the pool. Australia, Pakistan, West Indies, New Zealand, Sri Lanka and Bangladesh, with $128 million each, would receive 7.2 per cent each of the total allocable resources.[70] (Recall that Australia and England were the Big Three and see the disparity.) By no means could this be called a bad deal for the BCCI. (Geoff Boycott did not call it 'pure greed' anymore.)

Newspapers were also kinder and ran the following headlines: 'BCCI to Get USD 405 Million from ICC, Eng Next at 139

---

[70]Rao, K. Shriniwas, 'ICC "Hikes" India's Revenue Share; Bilateral Structure Could Undergo Sea Change', *The Times of India*, 23 June 2017, https://bit.ly/3Gg9lwK. Accessed on 18 October 2021.

Million'[71] and 'ICC Gifts BCCI a $112 Million Sweetener'.[72] Not a bad deal, at all!

Additionally, in the June meeting, we could get the home-and-away structure of the ICC reviewed. Member boards of the governing body were given the privilege to choose their bilateral matches. The BCCI, by virtue of being a member board, and most in demand for playing bilateral games overseas, could once again use this facility to their favour.[73] Also, our grievance of not being included in important decision-making groups of the ICC was redressed with India being included in the governance group and the all-important strategic working group of the ICC, which takes decisions on important commerce- and finance-related issues. The ICC also decided that it would not interfere in modalities related to bilateral agreement involving two nations. This was a major respite as the Pakistan Cricket Board had been constantly threatening legal action for 'not honouring' an MoU signed in 2014 to play bilateral games with them.

TIME FOR A NEW ORDER?

A seasoned journalist who has been a 'BCCI watcher' for more than two-and-a-half decades told me that the real issue was that once Manohar took over in the ICC and made his mind known

---

[71]PTI. 'BCCI to Get USD 405 Million from ICC, Eng Next at 139 Million', NDTV, 23 June 2017, https://cutt.ly/CP5y8fN. Accessed on 16 February 2022.
[72]Chakrabarty, Shamik. 'ICC Gifts BCCI a $112 Million Sweetener', *The Indian Express*, 23 June 2017, https://bit.ly/33g2Paw. Accessed on 14 February 2022.
[73]'Australia openly admitted that a visit by India meant a bonanza for that country. "We have a bumper year when India tours because the value of Indian broadcast rights are higher than for any other tour," James Sutherland, CEO of CA, told The Australian newspaper'. (Jaishankar, Vedam. 'ICC's World Test Championship Threatens BCCI's Financial Interests; Onus on Board, CoA to Stem the Rot', *Firstpost*, 26 June 2018, https://bit.ly/3qbtnTx. Accessed on 6 September 2021).

about the Big Three model being flawed, the sulking members of the ICC rallied around and nudged him to adopt a more equitable approach. This realization did not escape the seasoned and astute administrators of the BCCI. Knowing Manohar's bent of mind, and being privy to the trend of discussions in the SGM, they figured that the jig was up and they would only be waging a losing battle in taking on the other nations in the ICC. Saner voices in the BCCI, like those of Sharad Pawar, advising them in the SGM of 19 February 2016, brought home the fact even more clearly.

It was either those on whom the realpolitik of the situation had still not dawned, or those too committed to the ill-fated model, who continued to pursue the mirage of that model. The journalist concluded that it was convenient for all the dramatis personae, who had participated in the revamp of that model that the CoA came along to be the fall guys to take the hit of loss of revenue to the BCCI. A rather diabolical interpretation! But, I guess this was the observation of a journalist who had watched and learnt the ways of the BCCI for years!

The BCCI is by far the single-most important revenue earner for the ICC. This gives it huge clout. However, the wisdom is in being able to use its soft power in leveraging that clout and not being ham-handed. Firstly, the Big Three formula, even if it was financially beneficial to the BCCI, was very tactlessly introduced. You cannot twist arms now that the ICC has 14 members, with each having a vote which cannot be swayed merely by the resources BCCI can help them generate by including them in its FTP cycle. More importantly, as Sharad Pawar, with years of administrative experience behind him, mentioned in the SGM that the BCCI must help other associations grow the quality of their cricket and should take care of member boards that have stood by them. Finances are not all.

But in concentrating on the financial model and chasing the

revenue pie, the issue that the BCCI had lost sight of was that, it was the governance and constitutional change model which was depriving the BCCI of its clout. From being an important member among the 10 Full Members, the BCCI lost out big time when new members were inducted. The ICC had hitherto functioned on the 'club model' of governance wherein the existing Full Members decide on the admissibility of a new Full Member.

Admitting Full Members like Ireland and Afghanistan without the consent of the requisite majority of Full Members is akin to converting the ICC from a member's organization to a regulator. Including an additional independent female director is also tampering with the voting rights of the Full Members. This is a drastic change in the governance model and goes to the root of the character of the ICC as an international organization comprising member cricket boards instead of a supranational authority having the power to regulate its constituents.

The BCCI cannot afford to lose its pre-eminent position in world cricket by ill-advised moves which have a limited and myopic vision. There is a lot one can learn from the way in which Jagmohan Dalmiya leveraged the heft of Asian cricket by stewarding the shift of power away from the Marylebone Cricket Club (MCC) at Lord's to Dubai and the Asian subcontinent. The veto power was effectively checkmated. The roles played by Dalmiya, in addition to N.K.P. Salve and I.S. Bindra, are examples of sustainable moves which have withstood the test of time. I am sure the present clutch of more shrewd and tactful administrators are aware of the pitfalls and will learn from the mistakes of their predecessors.

4
IPL: THE NEXT TEST

The IPL is truly a phenomenon. As the cliché goes, 'You can hate it. You can despise it. Do what you want. You cannot ignore it.' There are vastly differing perceptions around it: is it a T20 cricket tournament? Is it a carnival? Is it a series of 'fixed' games? Is it steeped in corruption? It may be none of these, or it may be some of these. Nevertheless, it certainly is one of the most sought-after and keenly anticipated events in the calendar of every cricket lover.

Of course, the stiff upper lip, diehard and devout lovers of cricket in its most puritanical form have spent all their living hours decrying this format of the game. I ask them: is cricket what it was in the days of Sid Barnes, W.G. Grace or Don Bradman? All flannel. Three days of play: one of rest and two more days of play? And that too with the red ball only? If it is meant to be that way only, then why do we see a full stadia, and cheering and waving spectators at every IPL game, when on the other hand, we bemoan the fact that Test matches played in the conventional style and schedules are unable to attract spectators?

If cricket was meant to be for the true connoisseur who preferred only Test matches, fair enough, limit it to them. Why shed tears that not enough people are flocking to the stadium? Why introduce the pink ball day/night Test match to draw crowds over the evening? Cricket boards in every cricket-playing country around the world are facing financial stress as that form of cricket is no longer generating revenue despite TV viewership. The fact of the matter is that the IPL was never meant to be puritanical cricket. It was a totally revolutionary concept. The reality that it has caught and engaged the imagination of billions of cricket lovers around the world, is testament to the sheer popularity it has garnered for itself. The IPL was conceived around certain characteristics that prevail in the present-day Indian socio–cultural–family context.

> There were a number of guiding principles behind how we put IPL together. One was that it should reflect the characteristics of modern India. So, energetic, colourful, noisy, exciting. Two, that it should not compete with other forms of cricket, but that it should compete with other forms of entertainment. So, that's evening prime time view. Not only is India somewhat short in terms of supply of sports content, it's short in terms of supply of entertainment content. Apart from Bollywood, Lalit (Modi) and I agreed that we didn't want to compete with other cricket, we wanted to compete with soap operas. We therefore needed to create IPL in the image of a soap opera, so that if you didn't watch last night's episode, you're not in the conversation at the water tank next morning. So that's IPL for you. An entertainment extravaganza, architected [sic] for an evening of pure, colorful cricket wherein the family could sit around and 'chill' after a grueling summer's day.[74]

If the tournament has to be validated against these parameters, its performance over the last 14 episodes is certainly worthy of

---

[74]Andrew Wildblood of the International Management Group (IMG) explaining Lalit Modi's concept to the BCCI in Delhi in September 2007, from: Bose, Mihir. *The Nine Waves: The Extraordinary Story of Indian Cricket*, Aleph Book Company, Delhi, 2019.

approval. So, the IPL finally has emerged as a new feature, usually described as 'sportainment', which has appealed to the masses looking for 'affordable in-house' entertainment.

It is also distinct from orthodox cricket for the attire that is worn by the players—cool, tight-fitting T-shirts that militate against the sartorial state (cotton or wool) prescribed by Bob Woolmer in his book *Art and Science of Cricket*. Woolmer explains that batting forms such as the reverse sweep, which has now become a trademark in the IPL game, was the most unconventional.

> As a disruptive weapon it is almost unparalleled. When Dermot Reeve first used the shot against Ravi Shastri in a match between Warwickshire and Glamorgan, fetching the ball from the rough outside his leg stump and smashing it out of Edgbaston, the Indian all-rounder was so shocked, he complained to the umpire that Reeve was batting left handed [sic]… Similarly Brian McMillan used the shot to lift Muttiah Muralitharan out of the Nairobi cricket ground. In both instances, the rhythm of the spinners was rendered haywire.[75]

The other quality of the tournament is its management and conduct. It must be said, to the credit of the organizers Hemang Amin, the COO of the IPL in the BCCI, and his team, along with International Management Group (IMG), the IPL service provider, that they ran the best-oiled machinery which unfolds a match every evening, with double headers on weekends at different venues, for 45 days. No sun or rain, election or pandemic could come in the way of the juggernaut that rolls across geographies and cities. It has unfolded in South Africa, Sri Lanka, the United Arab Emirates (UAE) and, of course, in remote towns in India like Dharamshala, carrying tons of video-screening equipment to where can be a nightmare.

---

[75]Ibid. 169.

In all these 14 years, not one glitch has been reported. Thus, any pseudo proponent of orthodox, red ball, Test cricket decrying the IPL, besides being a hypocrite for the cause of cricket, cricketers and entertainment seeking populace, is seeking to occupy the high moral ground for the 'gentleman's game' merely to delude himself. This is not to deny that there have been 'conflict-of-interest' issues around the tournament, or that two franchises had integrity issues against them. But has cricket or the BCCI not suffered from these very issues around its other formats?

It is just not me who has written so much in favour of the IPL. In the words of former Australian Test captain, Michael Clarke:

> The IPL has been great for the relationships between countries. The environment around international cricket has become friendlier since the inception of the IPL, because players know each other better. Look at how Australia and India were at loggerheads in early 2008. A few months later Matthew Hayden and Ricky Ponting were leading the Australian representation in IPL franchises. Andrew Symonds played with Harbhajan Singh. More recently the Mumbai Indians had Sachin Tendulkar as assistant coach to Ricky Ponting, with Harbhajan Singh in the same team. The after effects of 'Monkeygate' didn't run very deep, did they? It seemed as the worst conflict in the cricket world at the time, but the effect of the IPL has been to iron out those differences and enhance cultural understanding between players from different nations.[76]

Clarke has so eloquently explained how the IPL has made India not only the most sought-after cricketing nation, but established beyond doubt the decline in the dominance of England and Australia from the cricketing calendar of the world, in favour of

---

[76] Clarke, Michael. *My Story*, Macmillan, Sydney, 2016, p. 215.

India. Earlier, to be accepted globally and also to earn a package, players used to yearn for a place in county cricket in England. Today, players around the world first ensure their place in the IPL before they announce their availability for other leagues. Sometimes, it holds true for them playing for their country too. The most outstanding example has been that of West Indies player Chris Gayle, who was content playing in the IPL of 2017 and did not make himself available for his country's tour of England. Another remarkable example has been that of Ben Stokes. He was barred from playing due to some infractions not related to cricket. That seemed not to have caused him too much of consternation as he earned $4 million in the IPL, and that too for a mere eight-week engagement.

ROOKIES ON A ROLL

While all this may be true for foreign players, how has the landscape changed for Indian players?

Before the advent of the IPL, the only domestic tournament for spotting talent was the Ranji Trophy. Ranji is hardly watched by spectators and does not get too much television coverage. Secondly, it is widely believed that the selection of players for Ranji is fraught with favouritism and nepotism at the state level. The selectors, or in fact the state association office-bearers, do not have much at stake, and so, sometimes, the most deserving do not get a fair opportunity.

In fact, we have heard some horror stories about how selections are made for players to represent district or state teams. A case that came to the notice of the CoA was of how three aspiring cricketers from Delhi, selected to play as guest players in the Ranji teams for Nagaland, Manipur and Jharkhand, were duped by the selectors. These cricketers had allegedly paid ₹80 lakh on the assurance that they would be selected in the Ranji Trophy teams of three states. They learnt, to their dismay, that they had been given fake selection letters. The CoA gave directions for a case to be registered and investigated.[77]

While the selection process for the Ranji Trophy is not clear, the talent scouts in the IPL have much at stake for their franchises, and the commitment to choose the best is paramount. The desire to excel in high-pressure engagements has given budding youngsters the confidence, which they so expertly displayed in the Border-Gavaskar series, Australia (December 2020–January 2021). Despite the 'not easily forgettable' drubbing of 36 all out at the Adelaide Oval in December 2020, it were the rookies and products of the IPL—Mohammed Siraj, Washington Sundar, Rishabh Pant and T. Natarajan—who brought the mighty Australians to their knees! The focus on players during the IPL is so intense that the best talent invariably gets picked. Rahul Dravid, former director of the National Cricket Academy (NCA), had the following to say about the selection of Rahul Tewatia from Haryana, who became a sensation after the 2020 edition of the IPL:

> Earlier, you only depended on your state association to select you for Ranji Trophy. Now, from a state like Haryana which produces so many quality spinners like Yuzvendra Chahal, Amit Mishra and Jayant Yadav, Tewatia would have had limited opportunities. So it's no longer limited to state associations.[78]

By playing alongside the best talent in world cricket, Indian cricketers have developed confidence and self-esteem, which was

---

[77] PTI. 'Police Files Case in Rs 80 Lakh Ranji Trophy Selection Fraud', *The Quint,* 14 March 2019, https://bit.ly/3tcBYqV. Accessed on 4 September 2021.

[78] 'Rahul Dravid on IPL's Expansion to Nine Teams, Rise of Rahul Tewatia and Natarajan, MI's Dominance', *Scroll.in*, 13 November 2020, https://bit.ly/3th8lVw. Accessed on 4 September 2021.

not forthcoming prior to the IPL. Remarkable rags-to-riches stories abound. Starting from the Pandya brothers who had humble beginnings in Vadodara, to Mohammed Siraj, son of an autorickshaw driver in Hyderabad (he was bid for ₹2.60 crore) and T. Natarajan from Chennai, who declared that if not for cricket he may have become a coolie—to name only a few. The IPL has had its own impact on the lives of many cricketers. Additionally, there have been players like Rashid Khan from war-ravaged Afghanistan and Sandeep Lamichhane from Nepal, who have found a new lease of life because of cricket in India.

The strength of the IPL is in its TV rights, its sponsorship events and its huge gate collections, and thus the handsome packages that the players, who get picked in the auction, are able to garner. Further, the huge revenues that the IPL generates for the BCCI has enabled the Board to become a strong force in world cricket, so much so, that it counts itself among the Big Three, and in 2014, came up with the non-sustainable idea of revenue sharing in the ICC based on the Big Three formula. For no contribution on their part in helping the BCCI to enrich its coffers, the office-bearers of the BCCI tried to twist arms in world cricket, riding on the riches that the IPL had ensured.

Just to provide the reader with an idea of the kind of money that the BCCI rakes in, here is a break-up: sponsorship of Team India by mobile phone maker Oppo garners ₹1,079 crore for five years; the successful IPL title sponsorship bid by Vivo earns ₹2,199 crore over five years; sponsorship rights for matches in India (Paytm) fetches ₹203 crore over four years; Star India pays ₹3,861 crore for TV rights for bilateral cricket in India over six years. All in all, the BCCI's annual earnings have jumped to ₹4,618 crore a year, with IPL media rights contributing ₹3,269 crore. Would such humongous revenue earning not give any Board a heady feeling?

OFF THE MARK

The 2017 edition of the IPL was the tenth edition of the tournament, and the first after the CoA had taken over in January that year. It had very interesting sides to it. There was a huge amount of animosity against the CoA as it had been installed after removing the key office-bearers. There were murmurs all around that since elected office-bearers were not allowed to function, the state associations would not cooperate with the CoA, thereby putting the 2017 edition of the IPL in jeopardy. The ostensible reason trotted out by some state associations for non-cooperation was that the BCCI had not released the requisite advance of ₹30 lakh to the associations which stage the IPL, and since they were starved of funds, they would not be able to host the IPL.[79]

Incidentally, the reason for non-release of funds was a direction given by the Supreme Court to those associations which did not endorse the Lodha Committee reforms. We were being told in hushed tones that the leading lights of the 'old camp' wanted to ensure that it was either their way or the highway, and hence the attempt to derail IPL 2017.

Quite frankly, we were not concerned, knowing full well that this was only a veiled attempt at brinkmanship to portray the CoA as being incapable of hosting the IPL. No association would actually want to forego an IPL match as, besides the clientele being deprived of the entertainment, there would be substantial revenue foregone by the association. The interesting feature was the fund position. In the CoA meeting of 8 March 2017, we were informed that, led by the Saurashtra Cricket Association, certain associations had written to the BCCI seeking funds for

---

[79]Das, Debdoot. 'IPL 10 under Jeopardy as State Associations Face Cash Crunch', *sportskeeda*, 2 March 2017, https://bit.ly/3qhu6Te. Accessed on 4 September 2021.

conducting IPL matches. Since to get a full picture, it's important to know the amounts released to the IPL-staging associations, Table 1 illustrates the amount remitted to the associations.

Table 1
Amounts remitted to IPL-staging associations from 1 April 2016

Association	Amount (in ₹)
Maharashtra	47,62,56,583
Saurashtra	42,66,97,149
Madhya Pradesh	50,99,84,152
Karnataka	55,62,39,174
Mumbai	59,60,80,993
Bengal	54,24,58,770
Punjab	54,28,44,586
Uttar Pradesh	63,21,35,685
Delhi	3,02,01,072
Hyderabad	18,48,17,065

Source: Annexure 1 of the second status report filed by the Committee of Administrators to the Supreme Court on 17 March.

Besides the fact that they had adequate funds to conduct the games, I also give below (Table 2) the funds available in their accounts:

Table 2
Balance as on 31 March 2016

Association	Savings Current A/C	Deposits	Total
Andhra	5,94,46,643	38,71,82,774	44,66,29,417
Goa	2,42,56,111	15,63,950	2,58,20,461
Himachal Pradesh	4,15,26,198	2,11,66,557	6,26,92,755
Hyderabad	1,84,45,852	17,82,600	2,02,28,452
Jharkhand	4,22,10,186	5,16,00,000	9,38,10,186
Kerala	42,68,679	1,00,00,000	1,42,68,670
Madhya Pradesh	17,11,924	116,53,62,378	116,70,74,302
Maharashtra	6,37,93,790	3,28,05,982	9,65,99,772
Odisha	50,37,319	87,32,661	1,37,69,980
Punjab			169,20,88,767
Saurashtra	75,56,761	212,83,90,303	213,59,47,064
Tamil Nadu	63,68,416	20,79,28,346	21,42,96,762
Tripura	2,13,03,546	178,53,43,202	180,66,46,748
Uttar Pradesh	7,31,07,467	57,79,77,695	65,10,85,162
Vidarbha	76,62,647	103,43,94,753	104,20,57,220

Source: Annexure 10 of the second status report filed by the Committee of Administrators to the Supreme Court on 17 March.

Notes: All figures in ₹.

The Associations whose details do not feature have not submitted balance sheets for 2016-17 to the BCCI.

The source for both is Annexure A-10 of the second status report submitted by us to the Supreme Court. The funds available with the Saurashtra Cricket Association may be seen.

Even though each day of dealing with the office-bearers was a revelation and the CoA had begun to understand and enjoy it, we were certainly not losing sleep over their attempts to try and disrupt the arrangements. To provide for any contingency, we had ensured a back-up venue for every venue being put in the schedule. Hemang Amin, the COO, was an experienced organizer of the IPL, and between him and the CEO, Rahul Johri, back-up venues had been kept in readiness. For the state associations who were trying to create a false picture of not being in a position to host the event as they were starved of funds, we ordered the release of this amount under intimation to the Court after all contingency plans had been discussed in the CoA meeting of 17 March 2017. Press Trust of India (PTI) reported the actions taken by the CoA on 30 March 2017 in the following words: 'Remodelling the IPL payment method, the Committee of Administrators (COA) agreed to release match funds to state associations before they host their first match.'[80]

By the first week of April, all arrangements had started falling into place. The media had expressed confidence that the event would be conducted as per schedule: 'While there are fears of a backlash, the fact that some of the state associations have shown a dilly-dallying attitude...the members of the CoA are not too concerned about the rumours doing the rounds in the cricket circuit.'[81] All loose ends had been tied and no room was left for any association to attempt to create, even remotely, any disruption.

The IPL was conducted in a manner befitting its stature. Being the tenth season of the IPL, spectacular opening events had been arranged at every venue instead of having only one gala opening event at the time of the inaugural match. The tournament progressed with clockwork precision. It provided the viewing population with some fascinating cricket and scintillating

---

[80]PTI. 'BCCI to Release IPL Match Funds Before Start of League', News 18, 30 March 2017, https://bit.ly/3HO5IhC. Accessed on 11 January 2022.
[81]Acharya, Shayan. 'IPL 10: CoA Exudes Confidence', *Sportstar*, 1 April 2017, https://bit.ly/3JZgTpE. Accessed on 4 September 2021.

entertainment. It required a handful of full-time professionals in the BCCI to ensure the success of the event. The seasoned administrators who were busy trying to impress the Supreme Court—despite being over 70 years of age and having been office-bearers for two consecutive terms—watched the matches from the ringside. And while they tried their best to prove that without them being in the driving seat the IPL could not be conducted, they were never found wanting in the clamour to grab complimentary passes in every game!

I must add that these games come with their own set of episodic experiences. One late evening, I received a call on my landline from a gentleman who claimed that he had just returned from an IPL game. His voice indignant, he asked me this: 'What kind of a citizen are you if you cannot even have the national anthem played before every IPL game?' He very loudly professed his patriotism while deriding mine. He even wanted to know if he would have to go to the Supreme Court to have the national anthem played. Realizing that he had had one sundowner too many, I politely told him that these games had nothing to do with a nation's pride as they were club matches and hence the national anthem had no place in such games. Very surprisingly, he accepted my argument and mouthed a couple of accolades before he put the phone down. So much for patriotism and Indian cricket!

There is one more interesting incident, related to the requirement to call for bids for the IPL TV rights, as the earlier 10-year contract was expiring that year. Considering that we were not an elected body, I was not in favour of seeking rights for another 10-year cycle, as I felt that it was the prerogative of an elected body to do so. On the other hand, a three-year cycle would not have been commercially viable for television broadcasters as they would have to commit sizeable capital expenses to undertake the broadcast. Thus, it was decided to go in for a period of five years which would be lucrative to them to make competitive bids and yet provide the incoming elected body an opportunity to rebid the process after the five-year contract.

With this as the guiding principle, in September 2017, IPL rights were auctioned in a transparent bidding process. Star India emerged as the highest bidder at ₹16,347 crore for a five-year period. This was double the ₹8,200 crore, which Sony India had bid for the expiring 10-year period. From the Sony deal, the BCCI had earned ₹820 crore per year. The Star deal brought in ₹3,269 crore per year. It made abundant commercial sense for Star India to bid that staggering amount, as in the 2018 IPL, the first qualifier match between CSK and Sunrisers Hyderabad (SRH), had seen a humongous number of 8.26 million concurrent viewers on Hotstar. I believe this is a world record for live streaming in any sport across the world.

KEEPING FANS HOOKED

IPL 2018 proved to be a greater success, what with the two franchises which had been disqualified earlier, smoothly segueing back into the tournament maintaining player cordiality and franchise integrity. The final between CSK and SRH, with the former winning by the skin of their teeth despite being labelled 'Dad's army' (because of the presence of many players in the 30-plus age bracket), showed the thrill and twists and turns that the event provides to its fans, thereby ensuring that it grows in strength and popularity every season.

IPL 2019 turned out to be an interesting challenge. 2019 was the year of the general election. The 2009 and 2014 editions of the IPL, which had also coincided with the general election, had been held partly in South Africa and the UAE. As early as September 2018, speculations had commenced, that since the general elections were likely to be held in April–May 2019, the

IPL would be conducted out of the country, considering past trends.[82] Such speculative news items were appearing at regular intervals and were not doing any good to the BCCI, the franchises, the players or the broadcasters. Besides, the Indian cricket-viewing population was becoming increasingly despondent.

Adding to all these factors was the insight we had got as per a KPMG study that, in 2009, when the IPL was held in South Africa, a total of 22,000 rooms were booked in that country, 10,000 domestic flight bookings were made and millions were spent on ticket, food, beverage, transport and merchandise sales. In 2014, when that year's edition was partly played in the UAE with the first 20 matches being hosted there, the IPL contributed AED[dirham]275 million ($75 million) to the UAE economy.[83] Should all these gains be allowed to another country with the added loss of Indian fans not being able to witness their prized tournament?

The CoA needed to make its own arrangements, consult with the government and the Election Commission, and take a decision at the earliest. To ascertain the government's willingness to support the event, I held a round of consultations with Rajiv Gauba, the then Union home secretary, Sunil Arora, the chief election commissioner and, of course, Arun Jaitley, the most ardent cricket lover, supporter and administrator in the government. I must say, to the credit of all these personalities, that whilst their primary commitment no doubt was the smooth conduct of the general election, which is a humongous exercise in itself, they all viewed the successful conduct of the IPL within the country also

---

[82]Rituparna. 'Reports: The whole of IPL 2019 to Be Hosted out of India', *CricTacker*, 22 September 2018, https://bit.ly/3fa67i7. Accessed on 4 September 2021.

[83]Tiwari, Manas. 'IPL Economy: What the Cash-Rich League Adds to India's GDP', *The Financial Express*, 22 January 2018, https://bit.ly/3Glssp2. Accessed on 4 September 2021.

as a matter of pride to the Indian establishment. They promised maximum cooperation as early as January, at a time when none of them had the foggiest idea of the schedule for the election! Their commitment to the IPL was very encouraging.

Based on this assurance and support from the government, the CoA, in its meeting on 8 January 2019, firmed up the logistical factors and issued a press release confirming that the 2019 edition of the IPL would indeed be held in India and that the tournament would commence on 23 March.

In deciding to commence the tournament slightly in advance of the usual calendar, we had two considerations before us. First, hoping that the election would not be held before the end of March, we were planning to finish a major chunk of the league matches earlier, so that only the play-offs would be woven within the election schedule. The other issue was the Indian team's participation in the ICC (50-over) World Cup which was scheduled to begin on 30 May 2019. To participate in it, the BCCI had to follow the ICC regulation that teams arrive two weeks ahead of the tournament. We also had to consider the Lodha Committee recommendation which prescribed a 15-day period between the IPL and the World Cup. On the other hand, we could not have advanced the IPL any further since some South African players participating in the IPL were busy playing ODI and T20 series against Sri Lanka. The last T20 was scheduled to end on 25 March. Any further advancement would have made it difficult for players in the T20 squad for the Lanka series to join before 25 March. Scheduling the IPL within all these constraints was quite a task for Hemang and his team.

On 10 March, the Election Commission announced the schedule for the general election. The elections were to be conducted in seven phases from 11 April to 19 May. Counting was to take place on 23 May. Sunil Arora had specified that three days before the polling day and two days after it, no match should be scheduled in a city where election was due. Within this stipulation, he was exceedingly supportive and connected us to Umesh Sinha, the deputy election commissioner, who was to oversee the scheduling as per these specifications. Sinha turned out to be a fine officer, who despite all the multiple daily crises that organizing a general election brings (and believe me, any election brings with it crises of the worst kind), was more than willing to guide the BCCI officers. Due credit has to be given to these officers of the Election Commission. So engaged were they in their tasks, that despite our eagerness that they get to see at least one match in Delhi, they could not take out the time.

The tournament proceeded without a glitch. The final between CSK and Mumbai Indians (MI) was played on 12 May and what a game it turned out to be. Mumbai Indians won the tournament on the last ball and by one run!

However, the IPL is not all glitz, fun and cheerleaders only. The franchises also undertook societal upgradation to contribute to creating a better society. For example, MI, in association with the Reliance Foundation, has committed itself to supporting and strengthening facilities for adolescent girls. In the 2020 season, seeing the success of the Women's T20 Challenge, the foundation announced that it would offer the best of infrastructure, training and rehab facilities to Indian girls. The Kings XI Punjab in 2015 had committed to eradicate AIDS from Punjab and changing people's mindset towards HIV testing and investing in treatment. The Kolkata Knight Riders (KKR) announced a campaign to make citizens aware of the alarming effects of plastic use. The Royal Challengers Bangalore (RCB) announced, and is pursuing, a 'Go Green' initiative. All these initiatives, founded on a desire to give back to society, have helped the IPL emerge as a well-regarded and sustainable sporting initiative.

NO SUBSTITUTE FOR PROFESSIONALISM

The IPL has the potential to entertain millions of fans around the globe and has turned out to be the most anticipated event every year. People plan holidays, journeys and family events around the IPL schedule. The IPL's success has energized other sports to try similar models such as Pro Kabaddi and the Ultimate Table Tennis leagues. The IPL has proven to be the most lucrative engagement for all players. Not being picked up in an IPL auction is seen as a disappointment for players.

On the flip side, the property has become so invaluable that maintaining its integrity is critical. We have repeatedly seen the soft belly of the BCCI reveal itself whenever stakes are high. The history of the BCCI speaks of so many instances wherein individuals at the helm believe that they are the institution. This is the risk landscape of the IPL. It is absolutely imperative that the IPL is ring-fenced in very specific oversighting parameters so that any scope for misdemeanour is precluded.

The major areas in which there has been malevolence and in which propensity for such misdemeanours still exists include conflict-of-interest issues, lack of independence and transparency, exploiting insider information for personal gain, inadequately delineated financial and procedural regimen, and lack of financial oversight.

The IPL is an important revenue earner for the BCCI. It contributes to about three-fourths of the revenue of the organization. This revenue is bound to grow as the IPL is poised to grow in size and popularity. The total annual income of the BCCI is upwards of ₹4,500 crore. Its staff strength is large. Besides its own institutions, such as the NCA, it has to provide for the amounts due to players, member state associations and former players. It also has huge tax obligations. Managing all these transactions requires a team of trained financial professionals. It was most surprising that till 2016, the BCCI and its IPL unit, did not have a full-time CFO.

It would be a fallacy to believe that a part-time honorary treasurer with a handful of executives in the office would be able to manage the financial transactions. It would also be very fallacious to presume that the pay structure of a CFO is too high for the BCCI to meet. It is a specious argument that high-paid executives such as the CEO or CFO do not deliver value and hence can be dispensed with. It is imperative that the accounting and financial dealings of the organization do not come up for any further adverse notice. The BCCI is facing that risk presently and may be staring at a lapse of fiduciary responsibility which it can ill afford.

There is thus a need to create a unit of trained administrative and finance professionals who manage the accounting and administration. Presently, the set-up is ad hoc and skeletal. While it is able to deliver, the inherent strength of the administrative set-up is neither sustainable nor professional. Hence the need to create a formal structure of experienced professionals.

Besides trained personnel, it also needs to have a well-defined financial and fund-disbursing policy. This was prepared by Deloitte and referred to the AGM/SGM of the BCCI for adoption but has not been adopted as yet. It is very important for the IPL GC to periodically review the financial procedures and policy manual. It is essential to verify if proper financial controls are in place and that existing policies/procedures are routinely updated. The GC must understand the organization's exposure to risk and actively manage that exposure. Any lack of oversight over financial controls will prove to become the most vulnerable aspect of the BCCI administration.

The IPL also has a history of malfeasance due to various vested interests. Those associated with franchises have often jockeyed themselves to administrative positions, thereby being in the role of regulator despite having interest in the entity to be regulated. Defining and detecting non-compliant behaviour should be a basic tenet to be followed with clear-cut, demarcated guidelines. While it is not a natural corollary that anyone who has held office for several years is likely to make decisions in self-interest, the risk does increase with prolonged association.

People with lesser experience on committees find it hard to question the actions of the long-standing and highly respected contributors to the organization. It is common for capable administrators to remain unopposed at the election of office-bearers during the AGM. As a consequence, they have remained in their role for many years. Their contribution to the organization is also well acknowledged, especially when the role is honorary. This security of tenure, coupled with the trust and respect of professional personnel and honorary elected members, induces a more relaxed approach towards dealing with conflicts of interest. It is a slow process, and as such, situations where a conflict of interest exists can creep up on everyone, unnoticed.

The BCCI has been lucky in that a well-documented conflict-of-interest policy with examples has been formulated by the Lodha Committee. It merely needs to be made a part of the regular management literature and practice. Irrespective of whether they are potential, perceived or actual conflict-of-interest situations, the prescribed policy must be made a part of the institution's foremost guiding principles. However, it needs to be emphasized that the policy should be implemented judiciously and not ham-handedly. Application of the laid down norms should be exercised with discretion. The CoA has requested the Court for recasting these norms. I have dealt with the details elsewhere in the book. As a routine annual feature, every employee and elected office-bearer must make a full declaration of any actual or perceived conflicts of interest.

The role of elected office-bearers and top management in

setting the tone when it comes to regulating conflicts of interest is critical. Demonstrating objectivity, transparency and integrity in their conduct and business is crucial to ensure that these values trickle down to the rest of the organization. Leading by example makes it clear that alternative means are not tolerated and will encourage a speak-up or whistle-blower culture when conflicts are suspected.

Regulating conflicts of interest requires setting the right culture of compliance. A strong compliance culture will incentivize the right behaviour, steer away from compromising on transparent decision-making and raise the right questions when in doubt. The opposite is also true. Poor culture will discourage reporting and drive away the very employees who disapprove of opaque and ambiguous business conduct.

I have consciously laboured on this aspect of governance for the BCCI due to the obvious potential and history of failures on this score.

CHARACTERISTICALLY UNORTHODOX

The IPL is the BCCI's most expensive property. The growing value of the IPL ecosystem has been valued at $6.3 billion in 2018, up from $5.3 billion in 2017. It increased to $6.78 billion in 2019 but registered a decline of 3.6 per cent due to COVID-19 in 2020.[84] It showcases Indian cricket and Indian cricket management as no other format does. At the same time, malfeasance and other imprudent actions by some office-bearers or franchises have created a negative aura around it. This needs to be dissipated. Not all teams have conflict-of-interest situations in their management.

---

[84]Duff & Phelps. *The Bold, the Beautiful and the Brilliant*, 2018, https://cutt.ly/nP5ukiM. Accessed on 15 February 2022; Duff & Phelps. *Embracing the New Normal*, 2020, https://cutt.ly/tP5uQv1. Accessed on 15 February 2022.

Not all of them indulge in match-fixing or illegal betting. Not all matches are 'fixed'. Not all of IPL is steeped in corruption as some self-styled purists would have us believe. Then why should there be such a negative mystique surrounding it?

The format has ignited youngsters' interest in the game like no other standard-bearer or proponent. The cricketing skills, athleticism on the ground and physical fitness that one sees in the high-intensity engagement over 45 days, really makes the adrenalin flow among the spectators too. The benchmark keeps getting raised every season. The expectations of teams, franchises and, above all, the spectators increase a notch higher every year. It has succeeded in bringing international cricket into the domestic space, where Indian rookie entrants get an opportunity to play alongside established, world-class foreign players. It has induced confidence among these cricketers which never would have come their way if orthodox Test matches had been the only avenue for them to progress. It has introduced cricket not only as a livelihood but as a way of life. It thus deserves to be made sustainable in the long run so that cricketers and the cricket-loving public of India continue to relish the entertainment it provides.

5

MAKING CRICKET WIN

It is the second day of May. As I sit down in front of my desktop to pen my thoughts about the NCA, I realize that today happens to be the anniversary of the foundation of the NCA—exactly 21 years old. It was inaugurated with a rather low-key ceremony, within the premises of the M. Chinnaswamy Stadium, in Bengaluru, by Rodney Marsh, the guest of honour. The ceremony may have been without the pomp and show that today's ceremonies have, but it was not lacking in high-profile personalities gracing the occasion. The first ball faced on that wicket was by P.R. (Polly) Umrigar, who drove S. Venkataraghavan through extra cover in his inimitable style!

The spectators were no less eminent. Raj Singh Dungarpur, a cricketer and cricket aficionado, who was then the chairman of the NCA Committee, G.R. Viswanath and Hanumant Singh were also present. Speaking on the occasion, Dungarpur said that this was 'the most ambitious scheme that the BCCI, in its long history, has undertaken'. He went on to say: 'There are dark clouds on the game of cricket at the moment but the silver lining is the establishment of the NCA.'[85]

While Dungarpur did not elaborate on the 'dark clouds',

---

[85] Krishnan, Sankhya. 'NCA Launched Amidst a Sense of Purpose', *ESPN cricinfo*, 2 May 2000, https://es.pn/33hRZB7. Accessed on 4 September 2021.

he certainly made it amply clear that he would not brook any demur against his viewpoint. A respected personality and a cricketer in his own right, Dungarpur was also a towering cricket administrator whose contribution to the game has been invaluable. Sunil Gavaskar, a legend in every sense of the word, has a place of his own in the history of Indian cricket. Gavaskar was a committee member and advisor to the NCA in 2000. Writing in a tabloid that year, Gavaskar commented that an NCA team should not have been fielded against a visiting Zimbabwe team, as there were other players who deserved to play the touring side more than the NCA boys. Reacting to Gavaskar's comment, Dungarpur said in an interview to the same tabloid:

> One gentleman being a member of NCA said the Academy boys should not have been given a game against Zimbabwe. Such people should either resign from the committee, or take it on, or fall in line. You can't run with the hares and hunt with the hounds at the same time.[86]

Reading this, Gavaskar went to the Cricket Club of India the same evening and tendered his resignation. When I read of this incident, my respect for Gavaskar went up a hundredfold—especially since in those days, no cricketer worth his salt could take on Dungarpur! The story illustrates the same timeless and unchanging constant in Indian cricket—you may be a cricketing legend, and thousands may come to the Brabourne Stadium to see you play (definitely not to see the president of the BCCI), but you better fall in line with the idiosyncrasies of the president.

I mean no disrespect with this narration. It is only for the limited purpose of making a point. My regard for Dungarpur,

---

[86]'Gavaskar Resigns from NCA', *ESPN crickinfo*, 23 December 2000, https://es.pn/3GE4rKd. Accessed on 4 September 2021.

who I am proud to have met, and treasure a photograph with, is also no less.

Like the illustrious administrators, the first batch of trainees at the NCA, which has been modelled along the lines of the Australian Cricket Academy, was an equally illustrious lot of cricketers who have excelled in the game and have represented India in practically all formats. The batch comprised the likes of Mohammad Kaif, Murali Kartik and Harbhajan Singh, who were already playing Test cricket for India. Others in the batch were of the calibre of Gautam Gambhir, Yuvraj Singh and Zaheer Khan.[87] These were a truly outstanding lot of cricketers chosen by cricketing legend Kapil Dev.

Sadly, there's nothing outstanding about the present state of the NCA. It continues to exist with archaic and pedestrian facilities which are unbecoming of the cricketing giant that India is. (When the CoA visited it, Diana pointed out that it did not even have a 'ladies only' washroom.) Team India is among the best teams in the world; the BCCI is the richest cricket board in the world. The BCCI is meant to be a colossus when it comes to pulling its weight in international cricket. It is also fancied to be among the Big Three of world cricket. We bring in 70 per cent of the revenues that ICC earns. Then why is our own academy in such a state?

A LONG WAY OFF

Just like all other issues concerning the BCCI, thereby hangs a tale—one that takes us back to the early days of the NCA's inauguration. The NCA was indeed the brainchild of Raj Singh Dungarpur. He and A.C. Muthiah, the then president of the BCCI, had conceived of the academy. The options before them were:

---

[87]Ramchand, Partab. 'First List of NCA Trainees', *ESPN cricinfo*, 15 April 2000, https://es.pn/3qj9XMq. Accessed on 4 September 2021.

- Utilizing the premises of the KSCA at the M. Chinnaswamy Stadium
- Using the premises of the Sports Authority of India (SAI) at Bengaluru
- Using the land offered by the Tamil Nadu government in Chennai

In 2000, the working committee of the BCCI authorized the Tamil Nadu Cricket Association (TNCA) and the KSCA to liaise with their respective governments and get a proposal for setting up the NCA. The TNCA came forward with a proposal of 50 acres of land in Chennai. The Karnataka government also agreed to the KSCA request and proposed a 30-acre plot on the outskirts of Bengaluru, in Alur. The allotment letter mentioned that the land was to be utilized for the NCA of the BCCI and the cricket academy of KSCA. The KSCA directly entered into an agreement with the government of Karnataka and offered 15 acres to the BCCI at a cost (the cost was not finalized since the proposal did not go through). Since the BCCI was keen on having an independent academy of its own and needed more than 15 acres, it decided not to pursue that KSCA's offer.

In 2008, the BCCI directly approached the government of Karnataka seeking land for the academy. The government (represented by the Karnataka Industrial Areas Development Board or KIADB) offered 32 acres in Bidadi Industrial Area on the outskirts of Bengaluru for which the BCCI deposited 20 per cent (₹384 lakh) of the cost. In 2010, the BCCI again approached the Karnataka government to relocate the NCA at Devanahalli in the rural district of Bengaluru as it was more convenient, being close to the new Bengaluru international airport. The government allotted a parcel of about 49.39 acres in Devanahalli and the BCCI paid the entire amount after adjusting the earlier payment of ₹384 lakh.

Though the KIADB had allotted the land, it got mired in legal problems as the landowners from whom it had been acquired challenged the allotment in the high court on the grounds that a cricket academy could not be construed to be an 'industrial purpose' (ostensibly, the purpose for which the land was acquired). During the year ending 31 March 2014, an interim order was passed by the Karnataka High Court staying the notifications dated 8 December 2011 issued by the KIADB for allotment of the land to the Board.

In view of the protracted litigation involved, the Board told KIADB that it was no longer interested in acquiring the stated land and requested it to refund the amount of ₹49.97 crore already deposited with it. However, the KIADB neither allotted any alternate land nor did they refund the amount.

Thereafter, on 13 August 2015, in a meeting of the NCA Board, it was decided that since the land was not forthcoming from the Karnataka government, moving out of Bengaluru was inevitable.[88] The Board felt that Dharamshala, Pune and Mohali could be the new options. Following up on this decision, the Himachal Pradesh Cricket Association (HPCA) applied to the Himachal Pradesh government on 18 August for a 50,000 sq. metre parcel of land.[89] However, on the next day itself, *The Tribune* quoted the state chief minister as saying: 'We will not give any land to the HPCA unless and until they take steps to improve their credentials and have a democratically elected body and convert back to a society from its present status of a company.'[90]

---

[88]Kombra, Srikant Kannoth. 'National Cricket Academy Likely to Be Shifted out of Bangalore', *sportskeeda*, 14 August 2015, https://bit.ly/3re9ydp. Accessed on 4 September 2021.
[89]'Will Dharamshala Lose Chance of Housing National Cricket Academy?' *The Times of India*, 5 July 2016, https://bit.ly/3FurxBC. Accessed on 13 January 2022.
[90]Chauhan, Pratibha. 'CM Rejects HPCA Plea but Keeps BCCI Option Open',

He, however, did say that the request could be considered by the state government if it comes from the BCCI president himself.

No such initiative seemed to have been taken for allotment in Mohali and Pune.

In November 2016, the KIADB came up with an alternate proposal for the BCCI, and offered 25 acres at another site in Devanahalli, which was free of any encumbrance. This was against the money already lying with them since 2010. This offer was not for an outright purchase but on a 99-year lease. The then president and secretary had reservations about the offer and felt that the BCCI should seek refund of its money. In fact, the then secretary had written to some select state associations seeking to know if they were interested in hosting the academy in their state. Some associations showed interest.

A NEW LEASE OF LIFE

In February 2017, a reminder from the KIADB (dated 21 February) to the allotment letter of 4 November 2016, caused some concern in the mind of Prof. Ratnakar Shetty (GM admin and game development), a very knowledgeable and experienced professional. The reminder letter stipulated that the BCCI needed to adhere to the time schedule prescribed in the standard conditions and take possession of the land within one month of the receipt of the letter. Obviously, this condition and the fact that the BCCI had waited for six years after paying the full amount to get an allotment made Shetty anxious.

Then through an email, Shetty, for the first time, apprised the CoA about the issues concerning the NCA since 2000. In

---

The Tribune, 19 August 2015, https://cutt.ly/RP5uPsx. Accessed on 4 September 2021.

this email sent to the three office-bearers and the CEO (it was the CEO who forwarded the email to us), he further informed us that the 2016 offer of the KIADB was awaiting a decision by the BCCI and if we did not act fast, they may withdraw the offer. He mentioned that the CEO, acting secretary and Niranjan Shah, the then chairman of the NCA committee, had seen the land and were in favour of accepting the allotment. Whether the then dispensation was inclined to accept the offer was not made known to us, but the unacceptability of the leasehold of the plot is on record.

The proposal was placed in the CoA meeting of 22 March 2017. It was decided that two of the CoA members, Diana Edulji and Ramachandra Guha, would visit the NCA and see the land on offer. In the next meeting on 12 April 2017, the CoA was informed of the suitability of the parcel of land on offer and it was decided to take possession of it. However, since 25 acres would not be adequate for an academy of international standards, it was decided to request the government for another similar-sized plot, appurtenant to the earlier one on a lease-cum-sale basis.

To ensure early allocation, I called the Karnataka chief secretary to request him to expedite allotment of the additional land. He was very forthcoming. The response which came very soon was that whilst 25 acres was not available, appurtenant to the earlier allotment, 15 acres could be made available. This offer was promptly accepted by the CoA and the additional plot was allotted by 15 July 2017 for a consideration of ₹37.50 crore, thus drawing to an end the saga of allotment of land for the NCA—a process that took 17 years!

However, former NCA chairman Niranjan Shah had a contrarian view on the matter and blamed the CoA for the NCA's decline:

> See, since the CoA took over, for three years, the NCA was totally neglected. They have talked about its development but never done any development. In my time, we at least purchased 40 acres of land near the airport and they (CoA) haven't done anything on that. They, also, unnecessarily disbanded the NCA committee comprising members who knew how to run the NCA.[91]

This made hilarious reading for the claim that they (Shah) had purchased 40 acres of land. And that the CoA had done nothing. Yes, I plead guilty to the allegation that we disbanded the NCA committee. But let's look at the considerations.

A plot of land measuring 25 acres was on offer from the state government since 4 November 2016. The CoA stepped in only on 30 January 2017. While the president and secretary had been removed by the Supreme Court on 2 January 2017, Shah continued to be the chairman of the NCA committee. Why is it that the land was not taken over immediately after the allotment letter came in November 2016? And in any case, how had they acquired 40 acres? The offer had only been of 25 acres.

The fact of the matter was that, the BCCI was not seeking an alternative site—they were seeking refund of the money deposited by them. They probably did not want the academy to be located in Bengaluru. In fact, if they had approached the KIADB after the high court had cancelled the earlier allotment in 2014, probably this very site may have been allotted.

I have narrated the saga of the purchase of land for the NCA; the rest is best answered by someone who has watched the BCCI and the NCA for more than a decade. Neeru Bhatia, a seasoned journalist, wrote in *The Week*:

---

[91]Charabarty, Shamik. 'Sourav Ganguly's Plan: NCA to Be Centre of Excellence', *The Indian Express*, 30 October 2019, https://bit.ly/3Go4HMZ. Accessed on 4 September 2021.

On December 12, 2017, the Committee of Administrators met at the National Cricket Academy in Bengaluru. High on the agenda was the need to transform the NCA into a world-class facility... But what stood out was the last decision: 'A ladies washroom/toilet should be constructed at the NCA and completed before January 3, 2018', read the minutes of the meeting... It is shocking that such basic facilities have been absent till now... As per information received from the BCCI, the ladies' facility was constructed on time at the NCA as per the instructions and efforts are on to make a larger one soon. The point is not about providing such basic facilities quickly. These should have been made available much earlier, by the cricket administrators who fiercely safeguard their domain and coffers.[92]

More need not be said.

MATCHING WORLD STANDARDS

The CoA was keen to conceptualize an academy which was world-class in every respect. It was meant to be a centre of excellence for all coaching activities, a rehab centre for injured and unwell players and a one-stop destination for all cricketing activities for the men's and women's teams. The infrastructure, as we saw, was terribly deficient. The NCA, which is meant to be the premium training academy in the country, did not have a full-time administrator, let alone adequate professional staff, to manage its cricketing activities, sports medicine, physio conditioning of players, etc. The support staff, in terms of physiotherapists, doctors, trainers, coaches—batting, bowling, fielding—was woefully inadequate. The complement of staff for

---

[92]Bhatia, Neeru. 'Women Cricketers Finally Get a Toilet at NCA!' *The Week*, 7 February 2018, https://bit.ly/3nl56s6. Accessed on 4 September 2021.

female players was even less. W.V. Raman was probably the only coach of repute in the entire set-up. The academy did not even have a full-time administrative head—a DGM of the BCCI from Mumbai was managing it on a part-time basis.

Generations of office-bearers had recognized that the premises, a part of the M. Chinnaswamy Stadium, was woefully inadequate. They had even felt that the NCA needed to be developed as a centre of excellence. However, nothing had been done even after land had been allotted and paid for to create the centre.

Following the CoA meeting of 12 April 2017, the acting secretary was requested to call a meeting of the NCA Board so that a joint discussion for engaging a Project Management Consultant and a committee to oversee the entire process could be considered. In the meeting of the CoA held on 7 August, it was learnt that the NCA Board had not met yet. It was then decided that the CoA would invite the NCA Board members for a joint meeting on 29 August 2018 in Bengaluru.

Meanwhile, the Supreme Court verdict on the new constitution was declared on 9 August 2018. On 21 August, the new constitution of the BCCI was registered. Once the new constitution was registered, all activities had to be as per its norms. Thus, all committees constituted earlier had to be disbanded. This was done on 23 August. It was in this context that the NCA Board meeting, scheduled for 29 August, was cancelled.

The issue facing the CoA was twofold. First, the existing academy, in whatever shape it was, had to be made functional to meet the requirements of a heavy cricketing season, which was on the horizon. The second was to start planning for a world-class facility that had been under discussion for 17 years but had not materialized.

The CoA reckoned that to set up the facilities, two categories of professional staff would be required: one would have to be purely administrative, to prepare a project, launch a request for proposal

(RFP), and see to the design and construction of the academy, stadium and administrative/residential complex. The other would be purely on cricketing aspects such as skills enhancement, training, strength conditioning, fitness assessment, recuperation, sports medicine and the like.

In accordance with this requirement, in the CoA meeting of 24 June 2017, it was decided to advertise for the post of project manager/COO for the NCA. A large number of applications were received. After the initial sifting, interviews were conducted, with CoA members and office-bearers present. After much deliberation, Tufan Ghosh, a top professional with about 30 years of experience in the healthcare and hospitality industry, having set up about 11 hospitals, was selected.

This selection was not without its own hilarity. Niranjan Shah shot off a letter to the CoA, claiming that the Court had appointed the CoA to supervise the administration of the BCCI, not to usurp it. He claimed that though he was the chairman, he had not been invited to the meeting.[93] I call this hilarious because despite a year having passed since the Court's verdict of 18 July 2016 disqualifying persons above the age of 70 years to be eligible to serve in the BCCI as elected office-bearers, Shah, at the age of 74, was still not willing to accept the verdict and was faulting the CoA for following the very mandate which had been entrusted to it by the Court. But then, that was the viewpoint of all the seasoned office-bearers in the BCCI who believed that they could function indefinitely, and other younger persons were not competent enough to replace them.

---

[93]ANI. 'NCA Chief Niranjan Shah Accuses CoA of Usurping BCCI Administration', *The Free Press Journal*, 30 May 2019, https://bit.ly/3rgJoqi. Accessed on 4 September 2021.

A PRIZED 'CATCH'

A challenge that remained was to get an outstanding former cricketer to head the training activities at the NCA to make it a world-class training establishment.

One of CoA's greatest 'acquisitions', if I can call it that, was persuading Rahul Dravid to join the NCA as the head of cricketing activities. Rahul was busy grooming the Under-19 (U-19) team and had produced some remarkable players. He had also made known to us the fact that he was too committed to the U-19 team and hence was not willing to take on the role of head coach of the Indian senior team. Since he was based in Bengaluru, which is where the NCA was located, we persuaded him to join the process that was being initiated to recruit a cricketing head for the NCA, and he agreed. We held interviews and he was no doubt the automatic selection.

One of the hurdles that confronted us was that he was on the payroll of India Cements Ltd. Hence, as a full-time employee of the BCCI, he could not concurrently be in someone else's employment. It would have been a conflict-of-interest situation. He offered to forego that employment for the period that he would be with the BCCI and produce a letter to that effect. This was accepted by our legal cell, and he joined. No sooner had he joined that a complaint was filed with the ombudsman-cum-ethics officer pointing to a potential conflict-of-interest situation. The complaint was heard and obviously dismissed. Rahul continued to perform a stellar role at the NCA till October last year (even Shah, in his interview to *The Indian Express*, lauded Rahul Dravid's presence at the NCA).

Meanwhile, the CoA was pleasantly surprised to see that the NCA was a subject of discussion in the SGM of the BCCI on 22 June 2018. How animated the discussion was, I am not aware, but the resolutions pertaining to it were very legally worded resolutions. I give the readers a flavour of the resolutions that were passed[94]:

> To consider and to take decisions on all matters pertaining to the National Cricket Academy, its programs, and all matters pertaining to the proposed new National Cricket Academy Head Quarters.
>
> RESOLVED THAT all decisions required to be taken by the National Cricket Academy Board in accordance with the extant Rules and Regulations of the BCCI as detailed hereinabove shall be taken only by the National Cricket Academy Board subject to any order of the Hon'ble Supreme Court.
>
> FURTHER RESOLVED THAT the National Cricket Academy Board is directed to examine and review the decisions taken in relation to the sphere of jurisdiction of the National Cricket Academy Board including but not limited to the processes and decisions of all appointments and conduct of programs, etc. which have not been done following the correct procedure and due process and to present the same to the General Body with their comments.
>
> FURTHER RESOLVED THAT the National Cricket Academy Board shall consult various stakeholders and devise programs making allowances for scientific progress in the field of sports sciences, future developments and growth and make recommendations for the requisite infrastructure for the new NCA facility to make it a state of the art facility.
>
> FURTHER RESOLVED THAT the National Cricket Academy Board be and is hereby authorized to take all steps to develop and finalise plans for the new NCA facility at Bangalore and present the same to the General Body

---

[94]Resolutions adopted by the governing board of the BCCI in the SGM at the Taj Mahal Hotel, 1 Mansingh Road, New Delhi, at 10.00 a.m., on 22 June 2018.

expeditiously to begin the work on the project in a time bound manner.

Somebody had surely taken a lot of trouble in drafting the resolutions. But to what effect? Unfortunately, there was no follow-up on it. I sincerely wish they had reached out and offered to assist in the planning for the development of the academy, under the guidance of the CoA, as had been mandated by the Court. The CoA received no further road map from any of the office-bearers.

On their part, both the professionals recruited by the CoA, went about their respective roles in right earnest. Tufan prepared a detailed concept paper and placed it before the CoA for a decision. It required floating an expression of interest (EOI) and releasing an RFP. Both activities would require substantial expenditure and commitments which would contractually bind the BCCI. By then, since the new constitution had been registered, the CoA had begun to prepare for the elections. It was felt that in the long-term interest of the BCCI, incurring expenditure on floating the EOI and RFP is best left to an elected body. The paper was thus prepared and kept ready for the elected Apex Council. That was the position when the CoA demitted office.

However, exactly a week after the CoA had demitted office, *The Indian Express* reported that the BCCI president, Sourav Ganguly, planned to make the NCA 'a centre of excellence': 'During Ganguly's felicitation at Eden Gardens last week, [V.V.S.] Laxman had urged that the NCA be transformed into a Centre of Excellence. If I have to make one wish to Sourav, it's just about how he can support, how he can revive the NCA. The greatness of the Indian team is its bench strength.'[95]

---

[95]Charabarty, Shamik. 'Sourav Ganguly's Plan: NCA to be Centre of Excellence', *The Indian Express*, 30 October 2019, https://bit.ly/3tlUEEB. Accessed on 4 September 2021.

This was an absolutely wonderful request. I was aware that former greats like Laxman were very keen to see the NCA develop and become a world-class facility. He had been a very accessible and cooperative member of the CAC, and other great cricketers like him had voiced that thought too. It has now been more than two years since this request was made and also more than two years since the CoA demitted office. I hope the NCA is taking shape and will soon be a world-class facility for our cricketers.

ICA: ANOTHER GIANT LEAP

It must be said, to the credit of the Lodha Committee, that it did a very comprehensive and thorough exercise in getting to the very roots of the issues that bedevil the BCCI. In its opening remarks, on the issue of the need for setting up an association of former players to espouse the cause of players, since they know exactly where the shoe pinches, the committee observed that an independent players' association be established since most Test-playing nations have such a body, and it was only the BCCI's reluctance that stood in the way of such a body's inclusion in the Indian cricket sphere.

This recommendation of the Lodha Committee was accepted by the Court and the constitution of the BCCI laid it down in its objects and purposes. The BCCI was enjoined with the responsibility of creating a players' association to be funded by it. It also directed the BCCI and its affiliate associations to have two players' representatives, one male and one female, in their Apex Council. As per the Lodha Committee report, an honorary committee of four members (the steering committee) was tasked to invite all eligible former cricketers to be members of the association. The four-member committee, as indicated in the Lodha Committee report, comprised:

    i. G.K. Pillai, former Union home secretary (chairperson)
    ii. Mohinder Amarnath, former national cricketer
    iii. Diana Edulji, former national cricketer
    iv. Anil Kumble, former national cricketer

For various reasons, the three former players listed above opted out of the committee. Since the committee had been constituted by a court order, the CoA recommended alternate former cricketers to replace the above three in its fourth status report of July 2017. However, the Court could not get time to consider the report, so the CoA set about constituting a committee on its own to complete the mandated task so as to facilitate an early election, or else two posts in the Apex Council would remain unfilled. We took the precaution of not flouting the court order and named this committee a 'working group'.

We reached out to distinguished former players who would not have a conflict of interest and also had the stature to set up the association. Fortunately for us, Pillai agreed to continue as chairperson, and Kapil Dev, Aunshuman Gaekwad, Bharat Reddy and Shantha Rangarajan agreed to join the committee.

It was the stature of Pillai and the experience of former players like Kapil Dev that helped in pushing the association through. Without the tenacity of the committee, ably assisted by Nandan Kamath, a senior legal advisor based in Bengaluru, this association would not have been a reality. No state association cooperated in locating former players, let alone agree to register their own chapters. Nandan helped register a Section 8 company and find three former players who could be the first directors of the company. Suitable articles of association and memorandum of association were drawn up, incorporating the model code to ensure that the players' association finds representation in the Apex Council of the BCCI.

Clearly, the association was registered in time against all

odds as no personality, other than those involved in the process, were interested in its formation. The association and the two representatives it would send to the Apex Council were seen to be totally unnecessary by self-styled administrators. After its registration was announced on 5 July 2019, there was disbelief of its having become a reality. I quote:

> A giant step towards the formation of a formal, first-of-its-kind Indian Cricketers' Association (ICA) has been taken by registering the body as a company. It is open to both male and female players... A body is now in place that will also have the approval of the Board of Control for Cricket in India (BCCI), which over the years had staunchly opposed all attempts to form similar associations and killed all such bodies ruthlessly.[96]

It beats me to understand why there was so much resistance to the formation of this association. Even as I sit down to pen these events, it is really heart-warming to read the news of the yeoman service being done by this association within just about a year of its incorporation. It is reported that it raised ₹78 lakh to help 57 former players (including a visually impaired player) who were afflicted with COVID-19. Legends such as Kapil Dev and Sunil Gavaskar helped contribute to this corpus. The body already has a membership of 1,750.[97]

However, as said earlier, there is never a dull moment in the BCCI. There was a news report quoting Ashok Malhotra, the first president of the ICA, where he is reported to have stated: 'Around 30 per cent of the 38 state cricket associations are not cooperating

---

[96] Ali, Qaiser Mohammad. 'Indian Cricketers' Association—a Welcome, First-of-Its-Kind, and "Official" Initiative', *Outlook*, 26 July 2019, https://bit.ly/34FGMe1. Accessed on 5 September 2021.
[97] PTI. 'Covid-19: ICA Raises Rs 78 Lakh, Extends Help to 57 Needy Cricketers', *Sportstar*, 20 June 2020, https://bit.ly/3rfUD2d. Accessed on 5 September 2021.

with the Supreme Court-approved Indian Cricketers' Association (ICA) by either not permitting the players' representatives to attend meetings of Apex Council or simply "not listening" to them.'[98] I hope the associations have begun to accept the reality and are now cooperating with the ICA.

This was certainly a major achievement. Cricketing nations around the globe have such associations which provide guidance to the national association on issues which directly impinge on the quality and well-being of active players. I hope that the association will continue to play a proactive role and their voice in the Apex Council will be heard. Hopefully, with newer blood coming in, there will be fresh thinking and a totally objective mindset.

---

[98] '30% of BCCI Units Haven't Accepted Players' Reps Says Ashok Malhotra', *Inside Sport*, 17 November 2020, https://bit.ly/3K6PJxj. Accessed on 5 September 2021.

6

UNCOVERING THE HEAD COACH SAGA

There are no two views that relations between coaches and captains, especially in cricket, are wrought with anxiety and tension. For a great synergistic relationship, a lot depends on how much each party trusts the other. In any sporting team around the globe, there have been more prominent spats than complementary roles with excellent understanding. In India, we have had the much-mentioned Greg Chappell and Sourav Ganguly episodes. Even Sachin Tendulkar had comments about Kapil Dev in his book *Playing It My Way* during his second stint as captain in November 1999.[99] Women's cricket has had its share too with Tushar Arothe and Ramesh Powar not finding the going good as coaches.

All the names mentioned above are legends in their own right but could not be comfortable together in the team dugout. Since history tends to repeat itself, how can it not be for spats between coaches and players during the watch of the CoA? We had our own share of trials and tribulations with coaches in the men's and women's side of the game. Let's look at the men's team first.

---

[99]Tendulkar, Sachin. *Playing It My Way: My Autobiography,* Hodder & Stoughton, London, 2015.

We were in Hyderabad on 5 April 2017 for a scheduled CoA meeting. That was the day on which, after overcoming many obstacles, the IPL was finally taking off as per schedule and the inaugural match was to be played. The office-bearers also attended a part of the meeting. During the course of the meeting, the CEO informed us that the head coach of the Indian team, Anil Kumble, only had a one-year contract and it was due to expire on 22 June 2017. This information hit us like a ton of bricks as we had no inkling of it.

The timing was exceedingly inconvenient since the Indian team had to participate in the Champions Trophy in the UK from 1 June, and from there, proceed for a tour of the West Indies set to begin on 23 June 2017. Considering the limitations of time and the need to provide some stability to the team, we looked at the terms of the contract and found that while his predecessor, Ravi Shastri, had been given a two-year term as team director, for some inexplicable reason, Kumble's tenure had been restricted to a year.

The CoA was informed that the BCCI GB had constituted a CAC for selecting the head coach. The three-member CAC comprised former distinguished cricketers: Sachin Tendulkar, Sourav Ganguly and V.V.S Laxman. It was learnt that the BCCI had followed a very elaborate and transparent process in 2016, post the expiry of Ravi Shastri's two-year tenure. It had released an advertisement for a new coach in the first week of June and received 57 applications, including Kumble's. However, it was reported that Kumble's name had not been included in the 21 names shortlisted by the office of the then BCCI secretary, Ajay Shirke.[100]

The CAC, however, asked for Kumble's name to be included. The committee had interviewed Kumble among other candidates

---

[100] Gollapudi, Nagraj. 'Anil Kumble Appointed India Head Coach', *ESPN cricinfo*, 23 June 2016, https://es.pn/3A84oU9. Accessed on 14 January 2022.

and recommended his name for appointment. Following the recommendation, the then secretary and president took the decision to appoint Kumble for a one-year period so that he could acquaint himself with the job and permit the BCCI to assess his performance as he had never taken on a coaching role before.

While researching to write about this episode, which is now history, I came across an article in *Firstpost* written by Tariq Engineer, who had the foresight to write the following, after the announcement of Kumble's selection in 2016: 'Kumble is effectively on probation for a year. The hope is that it will be enough, but the fear is that it won't be. If the latter comes to pass, Indian cricket will be the loser and the board will have no one to blame but itself.'[101]

I cannot help but applaud the accuracy of that prediction and marvel at the prophecy! The scenario, as it unfolded in the future, proved how 'spot on' that observation had been.

The CoA had been unanimous in its thinking that Kumble had a legendary track record as a cricketer, as one of the most successful bowlers of all time. He had displayed remarkable cricketing capabilities on the field and had the tough mental disposition needed to prepare the team for the oncoming ICC Champions Trophy. He had also guided the team to some remarkable wins during the year that he was coach. He was a no-nonsense coach and a brilliant strategist for the team. However, despite his credentials and track record, the CoA was legally and procedurally hamstrung in permitting an extension by simply taking a decision overriding contractual clauses.

Under the circumstances, without the contract having an extension clause, if the CoA had decided to grant him an automatic extension, there would be a cacophony of contrarian utterances

---

[101] Engineer, Tariq. 'Giving Anil Kumble Only One Year Might Make Things Tough for Coach and Team', *Firstpost*, 24 June 2016, https://bit.ly/3FtrW7l. Accessed on 2 September 2021.

commenting on the decision-making process being followed by the CoA. As a consequence, we were left with no option but to follow stated procedures.

In another CoA meeting held on 21 May 2017, in Hyderabad, in which the office-bearers were also present[102] (with the IPL final going on), Kumble made a presentation on the issues facing the players and proposed certain structural changes, including restructuring of payments and facilities at the NCA. It transpired that the players' compensation package had not been revised after 2011 though, of course, the CoA had effected an enhancement of the packages in March 2017 itself. He made some very good suggestions regarding upgradation of the players' compensation packages. During the course of the presentation and based on a query by him regarding his contract, the CoA and the office-bearers explained to him the non-existence of an automatic extension clause in his contract.[103]

Following this issue becoming public knowledge, a barrage of opinions appeared in the media. Some called his one-year contract a 'silly little contract'[104], which can be ignored by the CoA. There was also a cacophony of voices indicating that the players were unhappy with the coach's overbearing attitude—that he behaved like a headmaster[105], and it was also rumoured that the captain and coach were not on talking terms. Stories of dissonance in the dressing room aside, the issue was clear: for BCCI to continue to utilize his services, we would have to follow

---

[102]Ramachandra Guha (CoA member) was not able to attend this meeting.
[103]Minutes of the meeting of CoA, 21 May 2017, https://cutt.ly/1P5uJmH. Accessed on 16 February 2022.
[104]Sharma, Avinash. 'Anil Kumble Should Have Been Given Extension as India Head Coach: Lodha Panel', *myKhel,* 3 August 2017, https://bit.ly/3qxJTx6. Accessed on 2 September 2021.
[105]'Former India Coach Anil Kumble Talks about His "Headmaster" Tag', Zee News, 7 November 2017, https://bit.ly/3FuxhuR. Accessed on 2 September 2021.

a process. I cross-checked this decision taken by the CoA with a couple of persons who had been associated with the BCCI, as also legal experts, who felt that if we permitted a unilateral extension, it could lead to complications later.

AN UNFORTUNATE HIT WICKET

While this was being debated—more in the media than internally in the BCCI—Vikram Limaye, on the morning of 1 June 2017, called to enquire if Guha had informed me that he was resigning from the CoA. I had no such intimation so I dismissed it as media gossip. In fact, I was so dismissive of the information that I did not even call Guha up. Sure enough, a few hours later, the TV channels started announcing that he had indeed submitted his resignation to the Supreme Court. It was news to me, as I had not been aware of the issues which had made him take this step. I tried to speak with him, but could not. I sent him a text, to which there was no response. Sure enough, at 2.01 p.m., on that day, the following mail showed up in my inbox.

> From: Ramachandra Guha
>
> Sent: Thursday, June 1, 2017 2.01 PM
>
> To: Vinod Rai
>
> Dear Vinod,
>
> Attached [sic] my formal letter of resignation submitted to the Supreme Court today.
>   I shall be sending you a detailed letter/explanation shortly.[106]

We were aware of his strong views on issues such as conflict

---

[106] The letter he wrote to me subsequently is Appendix II in the book.

of interest, dominance of certain people on and off the ground, and also that Kumble should have been automatically given an extension. As for dominance of certain people—these were exactly the people who had thwarted the Court's attempts to make the BCCI adopt a new constitution. It was impossible to dismiss them easily.

As we have learnt in hindsight, it had taken nearly three years to get the states to accept the constitution, let alone the four months that Guha was part of the CoA. As for conflict of interest, the ombudsman is dealing with it. If all our woes could have been addressed by having a former senior male cricketer in the CoA, as Guha had suggested, we now have two in the Apex Council and, hopefully, Guha's concerns will be addressed.

It was a pity that Guha had not been able to find common ground with other members of the CoA and quit within four months. He had been very insistent that some national coaches had been accorded preferential treatment by the BCCI by awarding 10-month contracts for national duty, thus allowing them time to work as IPL coaches/mentors. And indeed, it had. Not only coaches, there were other functionaries who had been given 10-month contracts. We were cognizant of this cosy arrangement. However, any change in contract terms could only be done at the renewal stage. It isn't possible to unilaterally rescind a contract. The CoA took an in-principle decision, in June 2017, that BCCI functionaries would henceforth be offered two full-year contracts with no in-between window for them to engage elsewhere (read the IPL franchises).[107] But, by then, Guha had resigned. The norm was made applicable when contracts came up for renewal.

Other CoA members were also quite perplexed by his

---

[107] 'BCCI's COA Proposes 2-Year Contract, Ends IPL Stints for National Team Coaches', *Firstpost,* 13 June 2017, https://bit.ly/3A3lUsZ. Accessed on 31 August 2021.

resignation. None of us had any inkling that he was so disappointed. We wanted him to stay on to help us implement the task mandated to us by the Court. Nevertheless, Guha's quitting was unfortunate as he was an excellent resource with an in-depth understanding of the game and would have been an asset, along with Rahul Dravid, in remodelling the NCA.

The success of the CoA required us to stick together, complementing each other's strengths and pursuing the assigned objective single-mindedly. It was imperative that we function effectively as a team since all of us came from different backgrounds and had different perspectives on each issue. Interested parties were attempting to dislodge us and portray various negative perspectives in the media. We were grappling with the issues raised by Guha but four months was too short a time, considering the pushback. We had to be resilient and steadfast against these insidious attempts. Throwing in the towel was the easiest way out.

CAC: THE THIRD UMPIRE

Having taken the decision to advertise for the post of head coach, the attempt was to avoid a switch while the Champions Trophy was underway. We felt that while the team was preparing for the Champions Trophy 2017, an ongoing process would undermine the position of the coach and divert the team's focus towards speculations in the media. It would have created further acrimony. So we decided to announce the new appointment in the fortnight's gap between the tournament getting over and the team leaving for West Indies. The call for applications' timeline was decided accordingly.

In my conversations with the captain and team management, it was conveyed that Kumble was too much of a disciplinarian and hence the team members were not too happy with him. I had spoken to Virat Kohli on the issue and he did mention that the younger members of the team felt intimidated by the way he worked with them.

Newspaper articles and viewpoints in the media kept appearing to the effect that Indian cricket has become captive to 'superstar' culture or that now players (read captain) will be deciding who the coach should be. It is not the first time that teams around the world perceived dissonance in the dressing room. Dav Whatmore, the Sri Lankan team coach when it won the 1996 World Cup, and who has handled other international teams, such as Pakistan, Bangladesh and Zimbabwe in a two-decade coaching career (he was also the coach of the India U-19 team led by Kohli which won the U-19 World Cup in 2008), says:

> A successful coach is a good man-manager. You need to develop a healthy environment in the dressing room. You should give them good space and the players should have the freedom to express themselves. Of course, you have to have the tactical acumen and technical know-how to point out their shortcomings and address them in a diligent manner.[108]

He further added:

> Captains are powerful in every country and it is not just India. In India, you have to understand that these cricketers are superstars and they are treated that way... So the man willing to take up the responsibility of Indian coach has to understand the system and manage it.

All in all, I am also of the opinion that a coach can only be a friend, philosopher and tactical guide. It is ultimately the team and the captain who have to play the game, and it is on their

---

[108] Menon, Prasanth. 'Kohli-Kumble Fallout Due to Clash of Two Strong Individuals: Whatmore', *The Times of India,* 22 June 2017, https://bit.ly/3Ki9Ad6. Accessed on 2 September 2021.

performance that the team's fortune rests. After all, how many of us remember the team coach from when 'Kapil's Devils' won the World Cup in 1983?

The comforting factor for the CoA was that coach selection had been done in 2016 by the CAC, which comprised luminaries like Tendulkar, Ganguly and Laxman. They were towering personalities and were best suited to speak to the captain, players and the coach on how to go about the process in the future. In fact, when I met Tendulkar in Birmingham during the first match between India and Pakistan on 4 June 2017, I discussed with him in detail the awkward predicament in which we all had been placed. Apprising him of my conversation with the captain, I impressed upon him the fact that legends like him and other members of the CAC could bring about a rapprochement between the captain and the coach, and that maybe if it came from stalwarts like them, it could have the desired effect.

Tendulkar had seen the media reports and was conscious of the disquiet that was bothering everyone. He mentioned that the CAC would speak to Kumble and Kohli and ascertain the nature of the dissonance, if any, and factor it into the decision it would take in choosing the new coach.

Meanwhile, Rahul Johri and Amitabh Choudhary had a chat with the coach and captain. They felt that the differences were fairly severe and maybe it was only the CAC that would be best suited to have a thorough discussion with both of them. Soon, the CAC met in London and interacted with the two separately, in a bid to resolve the issue. After deliberations over three days, they decided to recommend Kumble's reappointment as the head coach.

FILLING JUMBO'S SHOES

While the decision of the CAC was still being conveyed, we received a bolt from the blue that Kumble had decided to step down as head coach. His Twitter message said the following:

> I am honoured by the confidence reposed in me by the CAC, in asking me to continue as Head Coach. The credit for the achievements of the last one year goes to the Captain, the entire team, coaching and support staff.
>
> Post this intimation, I was informed for the first time yesterday by the BCCI that the Captain had reservations with my 'style' and about my continuing as the Head Coach. I was surprised since I had always respected the role boundaries between Captain and Coach. Though the BCCI attempted to resolve the misunderstandings between the Captain and me, it was apparent that the partnership was untenable, and I therefore believe it is best for me to move on.
>
> Professionalism, discipline, commitment, honesty, complementary skills and diverse views are the key traits I bring to the table. These need to be valued for the partnership to be effective. I see the Coach's role akin to 'holding a mirror' to drive self-improvement in the team's interest.
>
> In light of these 'reservations', I believe it is best I hand over this responsibility to whomever the CAC and BCCI deem fit.
>
> Let me reiterate that it has been an absolute privilege to have served as Head Coach for the last one year. I thank the CAC, BCCI, CoA and all concerned.
>
> I also wish to thank the innumerable followers and fans of Indian cricket for their continued support. I will remain a well-wisher of the great cricketing tradition of my country forever.
>
> -Anil Kumble

This was vintage Kumble—mature, diplomatic and a thoroughbred professional. A legend in his own right, he has been a strategist on the ground with an outstanding work ethic. It is probably these instincts in his psyche that motivated him to step aside. As the elder statesman and the more mature member, he seemed to have taken this decision after he got to know that some team members had misgivings about his approach as a coach.

In a report published by *The Times of India* on 22 June 2017, Ganguly expressed helplessness in resolving the spat between the coach and the captain, and is quoted to have said: 'He (Anil Kumble) took the decision (to move on) at the very last moment... All I can say is that it was Kumble's personal decision to quit the post. We could not do much about it.'[109]

We had long conversations with Kumble after he had returned from the UK. He was obviously upset about the manner in which the entire episode had panned out. He felt he had been unfairly treated and a captain or team should not be given so much importance. It was the duty of the coach to bring discipline and professionalism into the team and as a senior, his views should have been respected by the players. He was disappointed that we had given such importance to following process, and that, in view of the team's performance over the previous year, he deserved an extension.

I explained to him that considering the fact that even his earlier selection in 2016 had followed a process, and that his one-year contract had no extension clause, we were bound to follow process, even for his reappointment. And that is exactly what was done. However, dissonance in the dressing room is not healthy for any team and since he, as the senior member, had decided to step aside, we respected his decision.

It is indeed very prudent of captain Kohli to have maintained a dignified silence. Any utterance from him would have set off a fusillade of opinions. Kumble, on his part, too, kept to himself and did not go public on any issue that had transpired. That was the most mature and dignified manner of dealing with a situation which could have become unpleasant for all parties involved. Many interpretations of the differences between the two have emerged. Many people have very authoritatively claimed to be privy to viewpoints of the captain and the coach. Suffice it to

---

[109]Bhaduri, Archiman. 'Anil Kumble's Decision to Quit Was Personal: Sourav Ganguly', *The Times of India,* 22 June 2017, https://bit.ly/3fxJdkY. Accessed on 2 September 2021.

say that each of them has been built on strands of information that were gathered from third-party sources.

Kumble's actions threw open the entire issue of replacement of the head coach. There were other qualified people who had taken it for granted that his reappointment was only a matter of following a process. They had, thus, not even considered it worthwhile to apply. The CoA considered this aspect in the very small window that was available to us and decided to extend the time frame for applications. This issue was discussed in the meeting of the CoA on 24 June 2017.

Diana felt that an extension of time frame should not have been provided and the CAC should have selected the coach from the remaining applicants. It was, however, explained that the rationale behind extending the date for receiving further applications was that some potential and deserving candidates may not have applied while Kumble was still in the fray. Diana wanted her objection to be recorded, which was duly agreed. As is the wont, among so-called cricket enthusiasts and self-styled experts, the extension of time frame for applications let off another cacophony. I reproduce a sample here:

> The BCCI on Friday extended the deadline to apply for the post of Head Coach till July 9, ensuring that a broader pool is available to choose from after Anil Kumble's acrimonious exit… The release states that applicants should be available for interview in person or via video conferencing by next week…[110]

Meanwhile, the team proceeded as per the FTP schedule to the West Indies, without a regular coach accompanying them. We sent an experienced professional, Dr M.V. Sridhar, a former first-class

---

[110] PTI. 'BCCI Extends Coach Application Deadline Till July 9', *The Times of India*, 23 June 2017, https://bit.ly/3tv9R6o. Accessed on 2 September 2021.

cricketer and an employee of the BCCI, with the team.

By 8 July, we had received 399 applications for the post of head coach! These applications were categorized thus:

1. Irrelevant applications: 104
2. Disqualified applications: 284
3. Eligible applications: 11

This clearly indicates that there is no dearth of aspirants for various assignments. One such instance is of a 30-year-old mechanical engineer employed with a construction company. He applied for the job as he felt that skipper Kohli was responsible for Kumble's ouster. He said he decided to apply as he felt that the 'captain of the team India (sic), Mr Kohli doesn't need a legend as a coach.' He goes on to explain why he is the perfect choice, 'Because I can adjust with arrogant attitude and no legend can do so and slowly I will drag (sic bring) him (back) to right track and then BCCI can appoint a legend as head coach.'[111] This only goes to prove the sentiments that cricket in India arouse. People take positions and are not shy of articulating them.

Meanwhile, the CAC decided that they would interact with six of the eligible applicants: Virender Sehwag, Phil Simmons, Richard Pybus, Ravi Shastri, Lalchand Rajput and Tom Moody. The CAC had been exceedingly cooperative in the entire process. Despite speculations appearing in public, we wanted to assure them that theirs would be the final word in the selection process and the CoA would not sit in judgment over their recommendation. I sent an email to the trio to assure them of the same. Inter alia, I wrote:

> While a mail from me on this issue is quite unnecessary, I mail merely to reassure you that the decision taken by

---

[111] PTI. 'To Teach Virat Kohli a Lesson, an Engineer Applies for Coach', *The Times of India*, 27 June 2017, https://bit.ly/3tsLUN4. Accessed on 2 September 2021.

you three will neither be influenced nor interfered with. The responsibility has been entrusted to you in view of the stature that you enjoy and the interest that you espouse of Cricket India. The responsibility under present circumstances is onerous but each one of you is more than capable of shouldering it.

However, the deliberation of the CAC was not to be without its own drama. The CAC met on 10 July and conducted the interactions. Ganguly and Laxman were in Mumbai, while Tendulkar participated via Skype. The media had piled up outside the BCCI headquarters, where the CAC was expected to make an announcement. To their surprise, no announcement was forthcoming. The CAC informed us that they needed more time to deliberate and also have a word with the captain, who was in the US at the time. Addressing the press, Ganguly had the following to say:

> 'We want to speak to Virat Kohli, once he is back from America, all three of us, the respective people concerned, we will explain to him that the coaches want to function in a certain way and make sure everybody is on the same page once we make the announcement. Once, we make the announcement, it has to be till the World Cup,' Ganguly had said yesterday [10 July 2017], indicating that the present stop-gap set-up might continue for India's upcoming tour of Sri Lanka.[112]

He also went on to say: 'What we have decided is that we will hold on for the time being (on) the announcement of the coach. We need to talk to a few more players, especially the captain,

---

[112] Pandey, Devendra. 'Announce India Head Coach Today: CoA Tells BCCI', *The Indian Express,* 11 July 2017, https://bit.ly/3I5TWzo. Accessed on 2 September 2021.

and then make the announcement, because we feel that there is no hurry at the moment'.[113]

Laxman had indeed mentioned to me that the CAC had made their choice and were proposing to recommend Rahul Dravid as a batting consultant for the team while it was travelling. They had also wanted to recommend Zaheer Khan as bowling coach. The recommendation of Dravid and Zaheer was okay by me, and the CoA would discuss and take a final call. That the CAC wanted to engage with the captain also seemed perfectly fine.

My concern was only in the fact that since the choice had been made, it would be unwise to delay the announcement as speculation would overtake and create avoidable confusion. Waiting for Kohli to come back from the US and then chat with him would have prolonged the agony and gained nothing. The chat could have been held after the announcement. And in any case, how difficult is it to speak to someone in any part of the world? Waiting for the captain to return and then hold discussions made no sense at all. It was going to delay the process by another two weeks.

The media was agog and had begun to make its own conclusions. It faulted the CAC for now wanting to consult the captain, which was contrary to the process the same CAC had followed in 2016. A news item went on to add:

> ...Somebody is trying to wash hands of this entire coach selection process, knowing where it is heading. The consensus on the candidate is clear. What someone is essentially trying to do is to put the onus on Virat and say 'we zeroed in on a (particular) candidate because this is what the skipper wants'.[114]

---

[113] Rao, K. Shriniwas. 'Virat Kohli Must Know How Coaches Work: Sourav Ganguly', *The Times of India*, 11 July 2017, https://cutt.ly/tPDBYEj. Accessed on 21 February 2022.

[114] Rao, K. Shriniwas. 'Onus Now on Virat Kohli to Pick Coach?' *The Times of India*, 11 July 2017, https://bit.ly/33qTAVt. Accessed on 2 September 2021.

The BCCI's clarification in the words of Amitabh Choudhary, the acting secretary, was:

> No decision has been made on appointment of new coach. The CAC is still deliberating over it. Irrespective of what various channels are running that's not the truth. The three CAC members are still deliberating. We are as eager to know as you are. Let's not put out things that are not true and not reached the stage of finality.[115]

I was not game for this prolonged process. That the captain and coach need to be on the same page is a no-brainer, and it had become all the more important due to our experience with the outgoing coach. Consultations with the captain could have been done on phone or video. Conspiracy theories were starting to emerge, putting the CAC in a delicate position.[116]

I told the CEO to inform the CAC that the announcement cannot be delayed. I was then informed that Ganguly had left for

---

[115] PTI. 'No Decision on Coach Yet, CAC Still Deliberating: BCCI', *Deccan Herald*, 11 July 2017, https://cutt.ly/AAsVm8z. Accessed on 2 September 2021.

[116] Memon, Ayaz. 'Ravi Shastri's Selection as Team India's Coach Marred by Power Battles', *mint,* 12 July 2017, https://bit.ly/3Ae7ztO. Accessed on 2 September 2021.

> Ganguly's explanations were shrouded in homilies and obfuscation. That the CAC and captain have to be on the 'same page' obviously stems from the Kumble fiasco, but is hardly a revelation. Moreover, that coaches have their own methods which the captain should be aware of was labouring a puerile point. Ganguly highlighted that presentations by all the candidates were excellent. While this would have made decision making difficult, this is precisely where a high-powered advisory committee has to live up to its task. Some conspiracy theorists say that all three members of the CAC had different preferences, leading to a deadlock. Others say that the CAC wanted to apprise Kohli of Dravid's and Khan's roles. Whatever the truth value of such stories, the rigmarole was unedifying. And the fundamental question remains: If the captain has to resolve the vexing matter, why keep him out of the deliberations in the first place? Indeed, why then should the CAC exist?

the airport and in fact taken a flight to Kolkata. That is when I had to give the ultimatum that the announcement had to be made forthwith. After he landed in Kolkata, the CEO apprised him of the need to make a timely announcement.[117] The BCCI then issued a press release to say that Ravi Shastri had been appointed the head coach for a two-year period.

But the painful saga continued. Laxman called to say that news reports were emerging that the CoA had reportedly given the impression that the CAC had exceeded its remit in recommending Dravid and Zaheer as consultant/coach. He called to convey the 'pain of the CAC'. I assured him that these were media speculations and somebody was quite unnecessarily adding his unsolicited two bits to the process.

The CAC was keen that we clear the air on this issue, which I thought was only fair. I clarified this aspect while speaking to the media, and the BCCI issued a press release expressing its gratitude to the members of the CAC and applauding their services which had been rendered most selflessly and on a pro bono basis. The fact remained that Dravid was far too occupied with the U-19 team to spare time for the senior team. Zaheer was contracted with another team and could not have been engaged. And hence that recommendation could not be acted upon.

That put the lid on the process.

There was no denying that the situation could have been handled differently. However, it needs to be recognized that the CoA was barely a few months into the business of administering the BCCI. In these months, we were beset with issues of the spat with the ICC, ensuring that the IPL is held on schedule and whether we should send a team for the Champions Trophy at all.

---

[117]Srivastava, Kislay. 'Vinod Rai Asks BCCI to Announce Coach by Today Evening, Ganguly Responds', *sportskeeda,* 11 July 2017, https://cutt.ly/BAsVV7k. Accessed on 23 February 2022.

Add to it, the fact that we got to know of the one-year contract expiring only in April and, of course, the serious recriminations that had broken out between the team and the coach. It was as a consequence of all these factors that events unfolded despite our best efforts.

7

THE MAIDENS BOWL US OVER

Hitting the headlines means you have arrived. This phenomenon holds true in all walks of life. No wonder when the controversy of the coach and a senior player in the women's team having a tiff came to the fore in 2018, Sourav Ganguly commented 'welcome to the group' to Mithali Raj.[118] However, to hit the headlines for the wrong reasons causes nothing but dismay. But champions are made because they have the ability to fight their way to the top and, despite challenges, remain at the top. Mithali is a true champion; she has been at the top for nearly 20 years now and has carried women's cricket on her shoulders in this millennium. She continues to mentor and lead the maidens from the front in the gentleman's game.

Ganguly made that statement because had also been at the receiving end of a disagreement with the then coach, Greg Chappell. Newspapers had enough and more to say about the issue, with every cricket aficionado having an opinion to air. Kumble had had to face it just a year before Mithali had her share of problems. Captains or senior players discuss and strategize every aspect of the game. Worse still, they always minutely analyse

---

[118]Ramakrishnan, Rahul. 'Mithali Raj vs Indian Cricket Team: A Blow by Blow Account', *mid-day*, 29 November 2018, https://bit.ly/3GEqXlS. Accessed on 3 September 2021.

the match they have just played. Differences in perceptions do occur. That is the beauty of the game. It is only when unsolicited opinions from outside jump into the fray, that problems arise.

The Ramesh Powar–Mithali Raj disagreement unfortunately took an avoidable turn. It landed on the table of the CoA, and before the CoA had even looked at the manager's report, a veteran sports journalist had put in his two bits: 'CoA Lacked Tact in Mithali–Harman Row'.[119] In fact, it was not even much of a Mithali–Harmanpreet issue.

So welcome to the club—again—where each one has an opinion and airs it freely before the scene has even unfolded.

The remarkable thing about the BCCI is the regularity and consistency of changes that take place and how they all come full circle. Tushar Arothe was appointed the coach of the women's cricket team in April 2017 for a two-year period. He took over from Purnima Rau, who, it appears, had to quit before the expiry of her contract.[120] Arothe had been the fielding coach of the team from 2009 to 2012 and had served as interim coach of the team for two tours, in May and June–July 2017. Questions were probably raised about his capability after the girls lost to Bangladesh in the Asia Cup final in Malaysia in May 2018.

What has now come as regret to me is that I did not devote enough attention to the women's team, other than appreciating their performance, till the finals in the Asia Cup. In fact, I had not even given second thought to the statement:

---

[119]Memon, Ayaz. 'CoA Lacked Tact In Mithali–Harman Row', *Hindustan Times*, 29 November 2018, https://bit.ly/3nudLbF. Accessed on 17 January 2022.

[120]Das, N. Jagannath. 'Players Need to Respect the Coach, Says Purnima Rau', *Telangana Today*, 16 May 2021, https://bit.ly/3KhEylk. Accessed on 3 September 2021; Purnima said: 'I was removed after we won the ICC qualifiers for the World Cup against South Africa in Sri Lanka in the finals with Harmanpreet (Kaur) hitting the winning six. They did not have the courtesy to inform me before they replaced me with Tushar Arothe.'

'CoA member Diana Edulji, a former India captain, is currently calling the shots as far as women's cricket is concerned.'[121] Former seasoned cricketer and then BCCI GM (cricket operations), Saba Karim, had the responsibility of managing women's cricket and it was generally accepted that he was doing the job well.

That my colleague Diana was aware of the goings-on in women's cricket and that the team management would seek her guidance from time to time, was common knowledge. I say this because it was Diana who informed me that the girls were unhappy with Arothe's style of functioning. This may have been immediately after the Asia Cup. I did not take it too seriously. However, she insisted that the CoA meet with the team to hear their grievances. We met them on 27 June 2018 to hear their side of the story. The team was represented by Mithali Raj, Harmanpreet Kaur, Hemlata Kala (chief selector) and Trupti Bhattacharya (team manager).

In the meeting, it was more the selector and manager who spoke about the inadequacies of the coach. They felt the coach was not up to the mark and had not been able to introduce any qualitative upgrade in the professional skills of the players. It was only after some encouragement from my colleague Diana that the players spoke about him not enjoying a good working relationship with the team. They also mentioned his inability to address the issues that the players were facing in terms of playing capabilities. It became obvious that there was a certain amount of misunderstanding within the team. We met Arothe on 5 July. He obviously felt that there weren't any inadequacies in his dealings with the team and that only a few were harbouring misgivings.

In the final analysis, it became clear that there was dissonance within the team, which never augurs well for any side. Obviously

---

[121]PTI. 'Indian Women's Cricket Team Coach Arothe Resigns after Players' Revolt', *The Times of India,* 10 July 2018, https://bit.ly/3GDuTUb. Accessed on 3 September 2021.

then, the players take precedence. Arothe decided to put in his papers. The entire episode did not leave a good taste in the mouth as the coach had more than a year of his tenure remaining, but the team was scheduled to travel and so an early decision had to be taken.

Applications were invited for a replacement. Of the 20 applications received, six were shortlisted after the preliminary interview. The interview committee comprised Diana, Acting Secretary Choudhary and Saba. Before the final interviews of the shortlisted candidates could be conducted, the Supreme Court verdict on a new constitution for the BCCI was declared on 9 August, which mandates that the women's team's coach selection is to be done by the CAC.[122] As such the committee, as indicated above, could not have conducted the interview.

The BCCI's first CAC appointed in 2015 included Tendulkar, Ganguly and Laxman. The members of this panel had reservations on continuing in the committee due to conflict-of-interest issues arising from the provisions in the new constitution as they had peripheral interests in some IPL franchises.

Meanwhile, since the women's team was scheduled to travel to Sri Lanka in September, a coach was urgently required. In view of the situation, a decision was taken to appoint the person most preferred among the six people shortlisted as an interim coach for three months, by which time the CAC could be reconstituted and the final interviews held. That person was Ramesh Powar, who happened to be working as the interim coach with the women's team after the exit of Arothe. The feedback from the players about him was quite encouraging. He was thus appointed as interim coach for a period of three months, till 30 November 2018.

---

[122]Perchance, the constitution is silent on the authority competent to select the chief coach for the women's team. However, legal advice was for us to follow the procedure laid down for the men's team, which required the CAC do the selection.

The team had the assistance of Powar as coach in its tour of Sri Lanka in September. Powar accompanied the team to the ICC Women's T20 World Cup in the West Indies in November. The team performed very well in the first four matches that they played beating New Zealand, Pakistan, Ireland and Australia.

The fifth game was the semi-final, in which they met traditional rivals: England. In this game, the Indian batting side seemed to collapse after the fall of the third wicket at 89 in the fourteenth over. The only batters who managed to score in double figures were Taniya Bhatia (11), Smriti Mandhana (34), Jemimah Rodrigues (26) and Harmanpreet Kaur (16). There was a total collapse after that with the team getting all out at 112. This was a rather modest target for the England team. They managed to score it with eight wickets in hand and 17 balls to spare. The match turned out to be a big disappointment for Indian cricket fans as the women's team was in fine nick and people had placed great expectations on their performance.

RIFT IN THE DRESSING ROOM

Our woes did not end with that defeat; in fact, it turned out to be the real beginning of our woes. All the newspapers carried the disappointing news. They also questioned the team management's decision to exclude the team's senior-most player, Mithali, from the match. This was all the more questionable because in the games that she had played earlier, she had managed to score back-to-back 50s.

To understand the reasoning behind such questions, we need to look at the team's scoring pattern in the games played before the semi-final.

In India's first group-stage match against New Zealand, we won by scoring 194 runs for five wickets and New Zealand scoring only 160 runs for the loss of nine wickets. In this match,

Mithali, who usually plays as opener, was to bat at number eight position. She did not get to bat.

In the second group-stage match against Pakistan, Mithali opened the innings and scored 56 runs and was declared player of the match. India won the match by scoring 137 runs for the loss of three wickets in 19 overs against Pakistan's score of 133 runs for seven wickets in 20 overs.

In the third group-stage match against Ireland, India scored 145 runs for the loss of six wickets and beat Ireland, who could only score 93 runs for the loss of eight wickets. Mithali opened the innings and scored 51 runs and was again adjudged player of the match.

In the fourth group-stage match against Australia, the team management took a decision to rest Mithali as she had a knee injury. India won the match scoring 167 runs for the loss of eight wickets and managed to skittle out Australia for 119 for the loss of nine wickets. In this game, Smriti Mandhana was the highest scorer with 83 runs.

In the semi-final match against England, the team management took the decision to play the winning combination which had beaten Australia—Mithali was not included in the playing XI despite her knee injury having healed. This was the match in which there was a batting collapse and India was knocked out of the tournament.

The main focus of India's defeat in the media was the decision of the team management to bench Mithali. Speaking to the press after the game, team captain, Harmanpreet, commented, 'We were going with a winning combination. We did really well against Australia. And that is the reason we just wanted to go with the same combination.'[123] One report quoted her saying she had

---

[123] 'Harmanpreet Defends India's Plan to Attack on Tricky Pitch', *ESPN crickinfo*, 23 November 2018, https://es.pn/326ZkTz. Accessed on 3 September 2021.

no regrets as the decision had been taken with the team's best interest in mind.[124] These statements by the skipper were fair as they merely explained the reasoning for the team management's decision.

Most unfortunately, what made the situation ugly was a tweet on 23 November by one Annisha Gupta, who claimed to be Mithali Raj's manager. Her tweet used some unfortunate words for the Indian captain and went on to add:

> Maybe I was a little angry but I think it comes from the right place because I don't stand for unfair treatment. The kind of favouritism that has been shown is very apparent. I think everybody can see the kind of favouritism that is being shown to certain members of the team.[125]

This kind of statement, from an outsider in public domain, is avoidable. While followers of the game have a right to their opinions, they should not indulge in naming and shaming. It is in poor taste to do so.

That was the first time that I decided to comment publicly on the issue and spoke to PTI:

> The comments made by people who appear to be associated with the Indian women's team have been viewed with concern. Such statements made in the media are totally uncalled for... The BCCI has a hierarchy of officials specifically dedicated to the redressal of genuine grievances of players... This is the appropriate mechanism that should

---

[124]PTI. 'No Regrets, Decision Was for Team, Says Harmanpreet on Mithali Raj's Omission', *The Week,* 23 November 2018, https://bit.ly/3tzvwdz. Accessed on 3 September 2021.

[125]'After Mithali Raj's Benching, Her Manager Lashes Out at Captain', *ESPN crickinfo,* 23 November 2018, https://cutt.ly/yAsBiWJ. Accessed on 3 September 2021.

be utilized… All players, the team management and persons associated with them must maintain decorum and follow the proper protocol.[126]

The GM (cricket operations), who is administratively responsible for women's cricket, as well as the CEO were advised to get a report from the manager, speak to the players and advise all of them to be discreet and not air their opinions in public. While this avoidable intrusion was yet to be digested, the headlines that caused great discomfiture to all of us was a statement by Diana on 27 November: 'Playing XI Cannot be Questioned', which stated:

> I think too much is being made out of it. The management (captain Harmanpreet Kaur, coach Ramesh Powar, vice-captain Smriti Mandhana and selector Sudha Shah) made the decision of not changing a winning combination and that backfired. If India had won the game, I am sure nobody would have questioned their decision, Edulji, a former India captain, told PTI.[127]

While the thought process of the CoA member cannot be faulted, a statement at that early stage, without getting a report from the team manager or the player concerned (at least I was not aware of any formal report as yet) was premature as it provided a lot of grist to the mill. One such person was the former coach, Arothe, who promptly jumped into the melee and faulted the statement of the CoA member, calling it contradictory, as he claimed she had questioned the dropping of another player in an earlier match.

---

[126] PTI. 'CoA Likely to Meet Harmanpreet, Mithali; Players Asked to Maintain "Decorum",' *Sportstar*, 25 November 2018, https://bit.ly/3fupcvJ. Accessed on 3 September 2021.

[127] PTI. 'Playing XI Cannot Be Questioned, Harmanpreet Kaur-Led Indian Women's Team Had a Bad Day During ICC World T20 Semis, Says COA's Diana Edulji', *india.com,* 26 November 2018, https://bit.ly/3nyPLUR. Accessed on 3 September 2021.

Diana says that (dropping Raj) is the team management's decision, so one cannot question (it). When we lost in the Asia Cup final, Pooja (Vastrakar) did not play…she asked me why Vastrakar was dropped? I told her that it was the decision of the team management… (Captain) Harmanpreet (Kaur) was there, Smriti (Mandhana) was there along with selector (Shashi Gupta), and we took a unanimous decision. Diana said, 'No, you should not have dropped Pooja.' I even explained that the reason we dropped Pooja was because she would drop catches in crucial matches…

I told her (Diana) the reason. She was like, 'You should not have dropped her. How could you drop her?' Now, she is saying that the team management's decision cannot be questioned. How can you change versions so soon? How could she question the team decisions (then)? Saba Karim and Rahul Johri were also there when Diana asked me this.[128]

I am not aware of the exchange nor did I pay any credence to the news items that appeared on the conversation that he was referring to. However, it set of a series of media 'breaking news' which served to further muddy the waters.

Meanwhile, the two players—Mithali and Harmanpreet—had separate meetings with Johri and Saba. Powar, the coach, also met with these officials. Mithali and Powar were advised to report to the CoA with written statements, which the media also reported.[129] It must be said to the credit of both players that they had not aired their views in public till then. Mithali and Powar

---

[128]Acharya, Shayan. 'Tushar Arothe Contradicts Edulji Statement on Team Selection', *Sportstar*, 27 November 2018, https://bit.ly/3I3hYeu. Accessed on 3 September 2021.
[129]PTI. 'Mithali Raj, Harmanpreet Kaur Meet Top BCCI Officials over World T20 Selection Drama', *The Economic Times*, 26 November 2018, https://bit.ly/33DB0ZY. Accessed on 3 September 2021.

both submitted their version of the incidents that took place in West Indies. As is the wont in the BCCI, before the CoA could lay its hands on the letters, they were all over the media.

Mithali had expressed her deep anguish at how she had been treated by the coach. She felt that more than her being benched in the semi-final game, it was the way in which she was being treated by the coach that distressed her. She even had to invoke the support of the selector to ensure that she continued to bat at her preferred opening slot. She expressed anguish in having been let down by Diana, to whom she had narrated the entire sequence of events after meeting the BCCI officials, and yet, Diana had given the media a statement alluding that the action of the team management could not be faulted. It had made Mithali feel that there was bias against her, which depressed and deflated her. She, however, made it clear that she had nothing against Harmanpreet, the T20 captain.[130] Powar, on the other hand, wrote a long report, the bulk of which was devoted to the difficulty he was facing in handling Mithali. He maintained that it was due to her poor strike rate that the team management had decided to drop her for the semi-final game and retain the winning combination of the last match.

However, these justifications did not go down well with experts and former players, who were genuine followers of the game. Gavaskar commented that a player of her experience should not have been left out of the semi-final. 'You have to pick your best player for the knockouts. You needed the experience and expertise of Mithali Raj.'[131] 'You should always remember you're [sic] best because you did something and there's an opportunity

---

[130]PTI. 'Mithali Raj Writes to BCCI, Accuses Coach Powar, CoA's Diana Edulji of Bias,' *Business Standard*, 27 November 2018, https://bit.ly/3rtdTcC. Accessed on 17 January 2022.
[131]PTI. 'I Feel Sorry for Mithali Raj: Sunil Gavaskar', *The Indian Express*, 28 November 2018, https://bit.ly/3ru8fY5. Accessed on 3 September 2021.

again. So I am not too disappointed seeing Mithali Raj being asked to sit out,' was Ganguly's views on the matter.[132]

TIME FOR STRAIGHT TALK

In any sport, there have been instances of misunderstanding amongst players and team management. It is natural. However, a mature and capable management will ensure that all such differences are sorted out internally. It is only when external interference is entertained that esprit de corps, or team camaraderie, breaks down. The fallout does no good to any side. It is the media and bystanders who enjoy revealing the 'scoops' and 'access to dressing room talk'. This is exactly what happened in this particular case too. While each group, with its own vested interest, was venting its spleen with comments such as the player's egos were more important than the country's interest, or the CoA was tactless, or that BCCI officials were settling scores by leaking mails, etc., the players were getting demoralized.

This was also an occasion for mischief-makers to contribute their two bits. I was being forwarded screenshots of purported conversations between outsiders interfering with team management and providing their advice/directions. There was a good deal of purported exchange being circulated on WhatsApp between a CoA member and the team management while the team was playing in West Indies. It involved the playing XI, the behaviour of the players and even batting positions. I discounted all this as loose talk since Diana had specifically told me that she was not on WhatsApp. There was no reason for her to hold back her

---

[132]Ramakrishnan, Rahul. 'Mithali Raj vs Indian Cricket Team: A Blow by Blow Account', *mid-day,* 29 November 2018, https://bit.ly/3fzibK5. Accessed on 3 September 2021.

WhatsApp number from me, so I obviously concluded that those messages were all contrived.

That outside interference was causing misunderstanding was soon realized by the players too. On 30 November, I was advised by Saba that the girls were keen to put the controversies to rest and close the issue. I admire Harmanpreet for reaching out to Saba and expressing a desire to have a frank talk with 'Mithali di' to ensure that no hard feelings remain, and all issues are ironed out. I was asked to sit with them. It was with a certain degree of trepidation that I agreed. The meeting was arranged in Delhi at a day's notice. The sincerity of both the players was evident from the fact that Harman drove six hours on a Sunday morning from her home in Moga to reach Delhi. Mithali, who was playing a league match in Guntur, flew in that morning. We met and chatted for over three hours. Quite a few issues were straightened out.

Harmanpreet, as the team captain, was clear that the decision had been collectively taken to play the winning combination. In this decision, the team selector and coach had been involved. She, of course, was not aware of when this news was conveyed to Mithali. On the other hand, Mithali felt that besides her exclusion not being justified, the manner in which it was conveyed to her had been most humiliating. She said that she had been kept in the dark about the decision and it was just before the two captains went for the toss that the coach had informed her.

It again is to the credit of these girls that, barring a reference or two to the coach, no other third person was mentioned. In the process, they also gave me some ideas pertaining to women's IPL and issues concerning women's cricket, which was very useful to me. While both the players had no grouse against the compensation package for the women's team vis-à-vis the men, they felt that training facilities and exposure to international teams needed to be intensified. They were very keen on a Women's IPL tournament as it would give young players opportunities to play alongside established foreign players and also bring up newer talent. Arrangements for travel and stay in various cities within the country and abroad also left much to be desired. There was some discussion on the poor quality of the kits that were being supplied to the women's team.

Diana was not included in this meeting. Maybe I should have involved her; maybe I was right in not doing so. However, none of the parties involved had voiced a desire for her inclusion, and so I decided to brief her after the meeting. I emailed her explaining what had transpired in the meeting and that I had encouraged the players to let bygones be bygones and settle their differences. She was obviously annoyed that I had met the players without her and true to her usual frank self, she emailed me back, emphatically stating that I was wrong to have excluded her. She believed that she could have used the opportunity to resolve some issues, since she had also been dragged into the controversy.

BCCI'S GAME OF 'MUSICAL CHAIRS'?

Much was made out of the fact that after the meeting Harmanpreet and Smriti had sent emails stating that they wanted to continue with the current coach, but there was a set of people opposed to this idea, too. The fact remained that Powar had only been selected an interim coach for a period of three months. Even if there was an extension clause in his contract, an automatic extension after so much of bad blood, did not appear to be appropriate. This was a view shared by many former cricketers.[133] Even if we had extended his term, the agony of dissonance in the dressing room would only have exacerbated. Furthermore, the selection had been done by a panel which had no legitimacy under the

---

[133]Gavaskar, Sunil. 'Calling for Powar's Extension as Coach Is Not Right Precedent', *mid-day,* 16 December 2020, Mumbai.

new constitution which stipulated that a coach selection is to be made only by the CAC.

The new constitution required the CAC to be selected by the GB, which was not likely to be convened soon. Hence, after taking legal opinion, an ad hoc CAC was appointed. Diana did not support this. She wanted Powar's term to be extended till the team's tour of New Zealand, after which a CAC could be appointed. However, when Kapil Dev, Aunshuman Gaekwad and Shubhangi Kulkarni were proposed as members for an ad hoc CAC, she opposed having Shubhangi in the CAC and wanted her to be replaced by Shantha Rangaswamy.[134] This suggestion was accepted. The new ad hoc CAC thus comprised Kapil Dev, Aunshuman Gaekwad and Shantha Rangaswamy—as credible a committee as it could get. I was very grateful to them for having agreed to join the CAC at such short notice, and help in the selection of the new coach.

The issue raised by Diana was that if Kohli could convey his unhappiness at the continuance of Kumble, and his words had carried weight, why not listen to the T20 women's captain and vice-captain and continue with Powar as the coach.[135] However, it is common knowledge that the decision on who to select as the head coach after Kumble's tenure had expired had been taken by the then CAC. It was left to legendary players to speak with Kohli and Kumble before they made their choice. The decision had not been taken by the CoA. True, the T20 captain and vice-captain (Harmanpreet and Smriti) had voiced their desire for an extension of Powar's tenure, but after so much bad blood had arisen between him and the ODI captain (Mithali), his position as

---

[134]Viswanath, G. 'Edulji Accuses Rai of Taking Unilateral Decisions', *The Hindu*, 4 January 2019, https://bit.ly/3Fvl3Cd. Accessed on 17 January 2022.

[135]Tagore, Vijay. 'If Virat Kohli Can, Why Not Harmanpreet Kaur: Diana Edulji. Why Not Mithali Raj, Counters Vinod Rai', *Mumbai Mirror*, 12 December 2018, https://bit.ly/3nxh0zj. Accessed on 3 September 2021.

coach had become untenable. And in any case, Powar had applied again and his application was also considered by the ad hoc CAC.

There was, of course, the continued insistence by Diana that in a two-member CoA, since the Court had not granted any veto power to the chairman, his opinion could not prevail over the other member.[136] I did not contest that opinion; however, as there was divergence in the instructions being issued by the two CoA members to the BCCI officials, they very rightly decided to take legal opinion on what course they should adopt. Justice B.N. Srikrishna (retd) was consulted. He gave a written opinion. It was only then that the CEO and GM acted on the instructions that I had given. The advertisement seeking applications for head coach for the women's team was issued on 1 December 2018.

The advertisement elicited encouraging responses. Experienced coaches such as Dav Whatmore, Herschelle Gibbs, Gary Kirsten, etc., as well as prominent Indians such as Manoj Prabhakar, Atul Bedade, David Johnson, Rakesh Sharma, W.V. Raman and Ramesh Powar applied. The CAC conducted interviews with the shortlisted coaches and decided to go with Kirsten. However, since he was already engaged with Kings XI Punjab, and BCCI rules do not allow dual responsibility, he backed out. Raman was thus selected as the coach of the Indian women's cricket team.

Raman joined in the first week of January 2019 and accompanied the team to New Zealand. Diana, however, felt that the entire process was illegal and that he should not be paid as per the new contract. Nevertheless, considering the fact that he had been selected and the BCCI had signed a contract with him, we were contractually bound to disburse his salary. The CoA discussed the issue once again in the presence of the new

---

[136]Sahi, Lokendra Pratap. 'Diana Edulji, Insulted "Equal Member" of the CoA, Hits Back at Vinod Rai with Vengeance', *The Telegraph,* 11 December 2018, https://bit.ly/3tvsGq5. Accessed on 3 September 2021.

member, Lt Gen. Ravindra Thodge (retd), who had, by then, been appointed by the Supreme Court. Diana held her ground. In the CoA meeting on 27 April 2019, she desired that the entire matter of the appointment of the coach be referred to the ombudsman for adjudication. Lt Gen. Thodge and I agreed. It was referred. And there it rests. Raman completed his term.

However, the story does not end there.

The changes in the BCCI going full circle continue to hold true. In 2021, the BCCI called for a fresh round of applications for the women's team's coach. Eight persons applied. The applicants included former India wicketkeeper Ajay Ratra, Hrishikesh Kanitkar and four women coaches, including former chief selector Hemlata Kala. Raman and Powar were also applicants.[137] After the interview, the CAC comprising Madan Lal, R.P. Singh and Sulakshana Naik, in May 2021, decided to recommend the appointment of Powar. Full circle!

All this was the sensational part of the story. It will obviously evoke a response from people who do not agree with what I have written. They will speak their versions. That is par for the course.

WOMEN'S CRICKET HAS ARRIVED

I now narrate the exciting journey that women's cricket has had in the present millennium. It is poised for greater laurels seeing the determination and mental make-up of the girls. I lamented early in the chapter that I had not paid too much attention to the women's team till the blistering attack that Harmanpreet launched on the Australian bowlers, despite having cramps and a torn finger ligament, in the semi-final at Derby in the 2017

---

[137] Gupta, Gaurav. 'WV Raman Sacked, Ramesh Powar Back as Coach of Indian Women's Team', *The Times of India*, 14 May 2021, https://bit.ly/3Gx9USO. Accessed on 3 September 2021.

World Cup.[138] With 20 fours and seven sixes, Harman finished with an unbeaten 171 from 115 balls—the highest score by an Indian woman in the World Cup. The Australians could have never predicted to be treated with such disdain or expected a battle of such proportions. It really made me focus on the potential that the girls possessed and I remember fervently praying for them in the finals, not so much for the laurels, but for the recognition they deserved.

It is thanks to the vision of Sharad Pawar, who was president of the BCCI in 2006, that women's cricket administration was taken over by the BCCI. It is widely acknowledged that Pawar as president of BCCI and Madhavrao Scindia earlier as minister of state for Railways, have played very prominent roles in the development of women's cricket in the country. The latter was instrumental in ensuring that many women cricketers got jobs in the Railways. It is to pioneers, such as Shantha Rangaswamy, Diana Edulji, Shubhangi Kulkarni and Sudha Shah, that we owe credit, for it was their passion that helped popularize the game and ensure that people in authority took note of its potential. They were genuine lovers of the game who staked much to ensure that participation in the 'gentleman's game' is not restricted based on gender. They often embarked on tours without really knowing whether they would have a decent place to stay or enough funds for three meals every day. They did not have a 'Board' to support them nor a sponsor of the kind that we have today, let alone television cameras following them. Yet, it was the passion for the game that drove their efforts and it is to them that women's cricket owes gratitude. From the days of players like Edulji, Rangaswamy and Kulkarni, travelling in unreserved compartments in trains, sleeping on the floor in dormitories and

---

[138]They had missed breakfast at the team hotel and not got any on the ground except oil-laden samosas!

canvassing for funds to sponsor the Indian women's team abroad[139] (when the game had not yet been taken over by the BCCI), to being permitted business-class travel in flights[140] (and a 'one-time benefit' of up to ₹30 lakh and a monthly gratis of up to ₹22,500 per month[141]), it has certainly been a long but rewarding journey.

Among the next generation were Anjum Chopra, Mithali Raj and Jhulan Goswami. The passion with which Mithali and Jhulan have pursued their love for the game is amazing. They have carried the baton for over two decades now and are still going strong. Playing in small towns with only parental support and no coaches or physios at their disposal, it has been a remarkable journey. Theirs is truly an inspirational narrative which will motivate hundreds of girls all over the country, with one being the highest wicket taker (Jhulan) and the other the highest scorer (Mithali) in women's cricket. It is so heartening to learn that biopics are being made on both these girls and soon the nation will be enlightened about their cricketing journey and how they have carried Indian women's cricket on their shoulders.

Now it is Harmanpreet Kaur, Smriti Mandhana, Ekta Bisht and Deepti Sharma who are the torchbearers for the game. A word needs to be said about the 'girl from Moga'—Harmanpreet—who has time and again asserted that she knows nothing else other than playing cricket. She has truly emerged as a sensation and is the cricketer to carry forward the baton for the next few years.

---

[139]Rangaswamy, Shantha. 'The Journey of Women's Cricket: South Asia's Sporting Mosaic', *IIC Quarterly*, India International Centre, Winter 2017–Spring 2018, pp. 44–52.
[140]Minutes of the meeting of the CoA, 17 March 2017, https://cutt.ly/SP5u1p0. Accessed on 17 February 2022.
[141]Minutes of the meeting of the CoA, 22 and 23 March 2017, https://cutt.ly/GP5u4rC. Accessed on 17 February 2022. This meeting took place seven weeks after the meeting in which the players' contracts for men for 2016–17 were concluded with a doubling of fixed component which had not been changed after 2011.

Her focus is single-minded, and her conviviality and esprit de corps in the dressing room are truly appreciated. These girls have brought the nation much pride.

Permitting the women's team central contracts in 2015 and initiating the Women's IPL in 2016 have been two of the most progressive steps taken to set the game on a more stable foundation. In 2017, the CoA decided to revise the annual retainer fee of the women players from ₹15 lakh and ₹10 lakh for Grade A and B, to ₹50 lakh and ₹30 lakh respectively, and created a new category of Grade C at ₹10 lakh. I was very pleasantly surprised to see Smriti Mandhana's interview that I would label 'mature'. She says: 'We need to understand that the revenue which we get is through men's cricket. The day women's cricket starts getting revenue, I will be the first person to say that we need the same thing. But right now we can't say that.'[142] Indeed, a very perceptive and objective comment. She has been very correct in her approach.

The year 2020 has been extremely detrimental for sports in general and it has hit the women's team very hard. It was very heartening to see the BCCI sponsor the Women's T20 Challenge trophy along with IPL 2020 in the UAE. That gave the girls a chance to play some cricket, and indeed they showcased their talent very effectively.

Women's cricket has its tales of discovery of fascinating talents from among families with the most humble backgrounds. Radha Yadav, the daughter of a vegetable seller, Veda Krishnamurthy, the daughter of a cable operator and the latest debutante, Shafali Verma, who often disguised herself as a boy to be able to play amongst boys, are amazing discoveries. All these constitute very remarkable stories. The Indian Railways has been the biggest employer of women cricketers as nine members of the cricket

---

[142]Dias, Anil. 'Unfair to Expect Pay Parity with Men: Smriti Mandhana', *The Times of India*, 23 January 2020, https://bit.ly/3Ki6rtw. Accessed on 3 September 2021.

team are still employed with them. With this kind of passion for the game motivating them, the women's team deserves the support and facilities on parity with the men's team. Any institution that ignores them will do so at its own peril.

The day when these girls will bring great laurels to India is not too far; they will soon establish their supremacy in world cricket.

8

OFF-THE-GROUND MISDEMEANOURS

The exit of Ramachandra Guha in June 2017 followed by Vikram Limaye[143] in quick succession meant that Diana and I were the only ones left to manage the CoA. We may not have seen eye to eye on some issues but on the critical area of ensuring compliance to the Lodha constitution and ensuring cricket continues to happen, there was no divergence. We managed with a fairly good understanding, though we did have differences of perceptions. I respect her for airing them. We discussed issues frankly. Perhaps, the issue that caused the greatest difference of opinion within the CoA was that concerning the #MeToo allegation against Rahul Johri, the CEO. It is also the issue that possibly caused the greatest dent in the credibility of the CoA.

Most readers would love to have me lay it all bare, blow by blow, in this book. However, the episode concerns too many individuals whose identities are best not revealed. The issue was of a grave personal nature, effecting too many careers and lives. Hence, it merits discreet handling.

---

[143]Limaye was the CEO-designate of the National Stock Exchange (NSE). He had to leave the CoA because the regulatory body, Securities and Exchange Board of India (SEBI), would not allow him to join without demitting his role as a member of the CoA. His leaving was a major setback as he was engaged in systematically upgrading the financial structure of the BCCI.

The events unfolded on 12 October 2018, when a journalist put out a tweet on her Twitter handle claiming to be conveying a sexual harassment complaint against Johri. The allegation pertained to the period of his previous employment, from a lady who did not wish to be identified.[144] The tweet, however, was withdrawn before midday of 13 October, with the assertion that it should not be quoted or published in any manner and that doing so would be in violation of that specific condition. Johri's first action was to inform the CoA of this tweet on the morning of 13 October. I asked him to explain the allegation and be on leave. His explanation was received in a week, in which he denied everything.

When I discussed this with Diana, she demanded his immediate termination on the grounds that, with such serious allegation against him, the reputation of the BCCI was being put at risk. Since she was very insistent, I offered to speak to Johri and get back. However, dismissing a person without even a prima facie case being made out against him and not giving him an opportunity to defend himself, would certainly be tantamount to denial of natural justice. Hence, I held back.

The next day, I consulted some senior legal luminaries including Justice Mudgal, who was associated with the drafting of the Vishaka Guidelines.[145] The amicus curiae, Gopal Subramanium, whom I had reached out to as well, happened to be in London. He was very kind to provide his opinion. He felt that even to appoint an independent inquiry committee, there should be a prima facie case established to justify its setting up. I shared this opinion with Diana. But she was steadfast in her view that the

---

[144] '#MeToo in Cricket: BCCI CEO Rahul Johri Accused of Sexual Harassment', *Hindustan Times*, 13 October 2018, https://bit.ly/3fCz3Qo. Accessed on 19 January 2022.

[145] The Vishaka Guidelines are a set of guidelines that were intended to ensure women's safety at workplaces. These were instituted by the Supreme Court of India in 1997.

CEO should step down. The distilled advice of people, who were knowledgeable in how such issues need to be handled, was that justice could be done—both to the complainant and the one complained against—only by an independent inquiry.

Some credible names were ascertained to hold the inquiry, including Justice Rakesh Sharma, retired judge of the Allahabad High Court, Barkha Singh, former chairperson, Delhi Commission for Women, and P.C. Sharma, former director, Central Bureau of Investigation (CBI). Diana did not agree to any such committee being formed and pressed on for the CEO's dismissal. She, however, helped by pointing out that Sharma was related to a legal retainer in the BCCI so there would be a conflict of interest if he were to be appointed. We replaced him with Veena Gowda, advocate and external member of the BCCI POSH (prevention of sexual harassment at workplace) committee. Meanwhile, two more complaints against the CEO surfaced: one pertaining to 2017 and the other of 2002–2003. These were also referred to the independent committee for examination.

The committee met a few times and viewed the second and third complaints. The first complainant did not come forward. Others who had expressed a desire to be examined were allowed to appear and state their case. All this while, the CEO continued to be on leave. The committee finally gave its report on 20 November 2018. In their findings, Justice Sharma and Barkha Singh categorically stated that the allegations against the CEO were false and baseless.[146] They opined that he should be allowed to function as CEO, as before.

Gowda found that no case of sexual harassment could be made out. However, she advised that he should undergo some form of gender sensitivity counselling/training as his conduct at

---

[146]'Rahul Johri to Remain BCCI CEO after Sexual Harassment Probe', *cricbuzz*, 21 November 2018, https://bit.ly/3IjsOgo. Accessed on 3 September 2021.

Birmingham had been unprofessional.[147] From the committee report, it was clear that all three members were unanimous in their opinion that no allegation of sexual harassment could be made against Johri. The issue that remained was around Gowda's observations.

The CoA. discussed the report. Diana continued to believe that Johri should not resume duties. I felt that it would be grossly unfair to penalize him for an alleged misdemeanour during his previous employment, which an independent committee had not been able to establish. Such an action, on our part, would not be able to withstand judicial scrutiny. Legal consultations were held. Legal advice maintained that since there was no consensus among the two CoA members on the action to be taken, and the independent committee had not found him guilty of the accusation, the CEO could resume his duties.

The CEO was allowed to join back.

Much has been written and said about this issue. It will continue to be talked about. I believe I took an administratively and legally correct call on the allegation. Ample opportunities had been given to the complainants to make their case. Enough was said and asserted by others who had an opinion—they were all heard by the committee. It is easy to decide to terminate services based on unproven allegations but decisions taken need to be able to stand judicial scrutiny. Otherwise, like so many other decisions taken by the BCCI, which have been narrated earlier, they come back to bite you. And often with huge pecuniary considerations.

BOUNDARIES OF MORALITY

There was more excitement in the offing, and it had nothing to do with the cricketing prowess of the team. Hardly had the sun

---

[147]Ibid.

risen in the year 2019 that Johri sent an email stating that on 9 January, Hardik Pandya and K.L. Rahul had appeared on a television show, *Koffee with Karan*, and made sexist and disrespectful remarks about women, which had not been received well in the media. He suggested issuing them a notice seeking their explanation.

We agreed. Diana was initially of the opinion that they should be banned for a match or two to show we respect women and will not allow players to be disrespectful towards them. They were issued show-cause notices seeking their response in seven days. Meanwhile, I discussed the issue with Ravi Shastri, the head coach, who was then in Australia with the team. Both of us felt that this was an off-the-ground misdemeanour, which should be handled by suspending them from playing a couple of matches and confiscation of match fees, if they were willing to render a sincere public apology.

So, the next day, on 10 January, I proposed a two-match suspension and sought Diana's opinion. She forwarded my email to the three office-bearers seeking the opinion of the acting secretary and sought in-house legal opinion. That started a fusillade of emails (reproduced in Appendix III). All the three-office bearers suggested 'strict action' as per BCCI rules. Thus, following the BCCI rules, on 11 January, the two players were placed under suspension. Both the players were in Australia with the team and had to be called back. Diana had made it clear that they should be kept under suspension till further course of action was decided for this misconduct, as was done in the case of the CEO, when he was sent on leave. In such disciplinary cases, BCCI rules require the CEO to conduct an inquiry, the report of which is to be given to the Apex Council who is to send it to the ombudsman for final disciplinary action.

However, Diana was not happy with the CEO conducting an inquiry and wanted the CoA, along with the three office-bearers, or the CoA along with the acting secretary, to do the inquiry. She was also of the view that we should not hurry with the inquiry as it may look like a cover-up job and quoted a precedent of when Lala Amarnath was sent back from the UK on some act of misdemeanour. She also mentioned in her mail: 'For your knowledge, in the recently concluded Football World Cup, a Croatian player was sent back after their first game on disciplinary grounds, and Croatia went on to win the World Cup.' However, since such an inquiry by office-bearers would not have been as per rules, I offered to excuse myself and told her to do the inquiry if she so wanted. I, however, did point out that it was France, not Croatia, which had won the World Cup!

Meanwhile, BCCI (acting) President C.K. Khanna, resiling from the position taken earlier in his mail of 10 January, sent us an email mentioning that it had been nine days since the players' suspension and that they sincerely regretted their utterances. He suggested that, pending an inquiry, they be reinstated and be allowed to join the team in New Zealand. His argument was that they are talented cricketers and were sure to be part of the World Cup squad, and so should be permitted. Sourav Ganguly was also of the opinion that, 'People make mistakes, let's not go too far here. I am sure, whoever has done it will realise and come out a better person. We are human beings not machines that we will always be perfect. We should move on and make sure it doesn't happen again.'[148]

Rahul and Pandya are among the finest we have in the team. Not being so media savvy, they seemed to have got carried away and indulged in 'boy's dressing room talk' without being conscious that they were on national television. We all acknowledge that their

---

[148] PTI. 'Hardik Pandya, KL Rahul Row: People Make Mistakes, Let's Move on, Says Sourav Ganguly', *The Indian Express*, 17 January 2019, https://bit.ly/3nElkNc. Accessed on 3 September 2021.

remarks were reprehensible. They regretted the same and tendered an unconditional apology. An off-the-ground misdemeanour of this kind needed a correction but did not require putting their careers in jeopardy. I felt that prolonging their suspension and keeping them away from cricket could possibly cause an irreparable scar on their career and make matters worse. Disciplinary issues are required to be referred to an ombudsman, but the BCCI did not have an ombudsman (he can only be appointed by the GB), and despite our suggesting a panel of names, the SGM had not appointed anyone. We had then requested the Court to appoint the ombudsman as his services were urgently required.

However, waiting for the court to appoint an ombudsman, have him take charge and conduct an inquiry, would have taken months. This was definitely not the course I wanted to pursue. It occurred to me that suspension is purely an administrative action. It had been ordered by the CoA and thus could be revoked administratively. However, knowing that my opinion would not have got traction, I had a word with the amicus curiae, who conceded that, pending the Court appointing an ombudsman, the suspension could certainly be revoked. He spoke to Diana, who agreed. I concurred too! The players were reinstated on 24 January. Hardik flew back to New Zealand to join the team and Rahul joined India A, who were playing against the England Lions in India.

D.K. Jain was appointed ombudsman and an inquiry was conducted. He sought the opinion of the CoA. I requested Johri to inform him that the CoA felt that the penalty levied on the players, i.e. loss of match fee and the punishment of sitting out five games, was sufficient punishment for their misdemeanour. Finally, it was on 21 April that the ombudsman could give his verdict, and he fined them ₹20 lakh each. This ended the saga. Fortunately, the players, who had expressed remorse, were able to be active on the field after 21 January 2019 itself!

9
ON THE FRONT FOOT

Early on in my innings, I had to deal with the controversy surrounding the participation of the team in the ICC Champions Trophy 2017. Little did I realize then that there would be many more such controversies that would keep my colleague and me on our toes.

Of these, the issue that led to rising tempers and sharp reactions from certain quarters was our response to the Pulwama attack, and the contentious question: should India boycott Pakistan in the 2019 World Cup?

Why was the question being asked? On 14 February 2019, a suicide bomber belonging to the Jaish-e-Mohammed (JeM) had crashed a car packed with explosives into a convoy of the Central Reserve Police Force (CRPF) killing more than 40 Indian paramilitary personnel and injuring at least 70. The dastardly attack took place in Pulwama, about 20 kilometres from Srinagar. It was an act of extreme cowardice, executed on a set of unsuspecting paramilitary personnel who were travelling from one city to another. It wiped out breadwinners from scores of families. The stories one heard were heart-rending. The origin of the initiative and planning of the heinous act was well known. The attack had been globally denounced by all countries. India had announced various retaliatory measures which, inter alia, involved revoking Pakistan's most favoured nation (MFN) status in trade, and increasing customs duty on imports to 200 per cent.

Tempers were running high. Since cricket in India is not considered just a game—it is a religion—and citizens consider it to represent 'Indianness' in every respect, the sport somehow becomes the focal point whenever relations between the two countries dip. As luck would have it, the draw for the World Cup matches was announced on 20 February, and as per that draw, India was scheduled to play Pakistan on 16 June.

As soon as the draw was announced, the BCCI became the favourite whipping boy. Every channel was decrying the BCCI, screaming that it was putting its revenue interests before the nation. The BCCI (read CoA) was being termed unpatriotic and 'unfeeling' towards the Pulwama martyrs. This was despite the fact that at the height of the tensions during the Kargil War, in 1999, that year's World Cup had seen the traditional rivals clash and India emerge a winner.

Soon, the country began witnessing widespread protests in any manner that an individual or institution could register protest. Understandably, people had worked themselves into a frenzy and BCCI bashing was rampant. The Cricket Centre, a part of the Wankhede Stadium, housing the BCCI office, had to pull down all the photos of Pakistani players in the photo gallery. The Cricket Club of India, housed in the Brabourne Stadium, took particular care to remove the photo of former Pakistan captain and present prime minister, Imran Khan. For days, there was a collection of media crew wanting to go into the office and satisfy themselves and their viewing public, that we did not have any photo or memorabilia which could even remotely be associated with Pakistan. State associations had also followed suit. The stadium in Mohali, Punjab, a state on the western border of India and sharing a border with Pakistan, pulled down all photos of matches with Pakistan. These gestures were the result of mass outrage and anger across the country.

The sentiments sweeping the nation were so strong that DSport, the official broadcasters of the Pakistan Super League (PSL) being played in the UAE, were forced to suspend their telecast of the tournament. DSport blacked out their broadcast for the entire fourth season of the league. Reacting to this, the Pakistan Cricket Board (PCB) called the actions taken in India as 'regrettable' and wished to raise it with the BCCI during the course of the next ICC meeting. IMG Reliance (now known as RISE Worldwide Ltd), the official production company of the T20 League, reneged on their agreement with the PCB to live produce the tournament. *Cricbuzz* also suspended their coverage of the league games and removed the score card and other match details from their site.[149] Understandably, all this led to a virtual war on the internet and social media was abuzz with all hues of opinions.

By 22 February, this outrage had reached my doorstep. Very early that morning, I opened my front door to leave for a game of tennis. Imagine my shock when I saw a TV reporter with a mike and camera ready on the landing. He was pleading that I must give him a byte on the 'raging controversy' (as he referred to it) or else his editor would not let him enter the office!

The startling fact was that this was four months before the Word Cup was scheduled to start. There was enough time to take an informed decision after wide consultation with all stakeholders, particularly the government. However, the media had called upon the CoA to take a view and take it fast. Not only take it fast but make it known, too.

The attack had indeed been dastardly. Those in power in the corridors of the government must have been debating the best

---

[149] Oinam, Jayanta. 'Should India Play Pakistan in 2019 Cricket World Cup?' *Outlook*, 20 February 2019, https://cutt.ly/QP6cjSK. Accessed on 3 September 2021.

course of action to repulse such an act. However, as far as the BCCI was concerned, one of the questions being asked was should we give Pakistan a walk over when we come up against them in the league matches. One of our most successful off-spinner, Harbhajan Singh, speaking to a channel, said: 'Country comes first… Cricket or hockey or any sport, it should be kept aside as this is a huge thing and repeatedly our soldiers are killed. We should stand with our country. Cricket or hockey or any sport, we don't need to play with them.'[150] He certainly had a valid view which needed to be factored in.

On the other hand, there was a huge groundswell of opinion aghast at the mere possibility of an India–Pakistan match not happening. Such matches bring out the best in the two teams and keep spectators at their expectant best; it draws huge crowds and are eagerly awaited. However, in the cacophony that was unfolding, sane voices stayed mum and below the radar. Two of our most famous cricketers and legends of the game, Sachin Tendulkar and Kapil Dev, both lent their voices in support of India not forfeiting the match.

'India has always come up trumps against Pakistan in the World Cup. Time to beat them once again. Would personally hate to give them two points and help them in the tournament… Having said that, for me India always comes first, so whatever my country decides, I will back that decision with all my heart,' said Tendulkar. Former captain Kapil Dev insisted that the decision to play was not to be taken by former cricketers, but by the government. His take: 'It's better if we don't give an opinion and leave it to the government and concerned people. Whatever they decide will be in the interest of the nation. We'll do what

---

[150] PTI. 'India Shouldn't Play Pakistan in World Cup: Harbhajan', *The Week*, 18 February 2019, https://bit.ly/33OP037. Accessed on 3 September 2021.

they want [sic].'¹⁵¹

However, such was the frenzy in those times that even Tendulkar, who is revered as the God of Indian cricket, was trolled for voicing his opinion in favour of playing. Arnab Goswami of Republic TV insinuated that people who held Tendulkar's view were 'anti-national'.¹⁵²

The issue that deserved consideration was not the points in the league games but the fact that boycotting Pakistan in the qualifiers could cost us the cup. In the past, there had been instances when certain teams, for valid reasons, had decided to walk away from playing, such as in the 1996 series in Sri Lanka, Australia and West Indies had decided not to participate, citing security reasons as Colombo had just suffered a major blast. The teams had had the support of their respective governments, but in accordance with ICC rules, points were awarded to the Sri Lankan team. Similarly, in 2003, England had refused to travel to Zimbabwe citing security reasons and lost points.

So, if India was to give Pakistan a walk over in the Manchester game, we would lose points in the league table. This was not very critical as we could still reach the play-off stage; however, could we afford to boycott playing Pakistan if we came up against them in the semi-final or final, if Pakistan were to reach that stage? That would mean forgoing the cup. India was a team largely fancied to be a strong contender for the championship, so why forego the opportunity? The team had also prepared so single-mindedly for the tournament, a boycott was like shooting ourselves in the foot.

---

¹⁵¹'From Gavaskar to Tendulkar, What Cricketers Have Said about India Playing Pakistan at the World Cup', *Scroll.in,* 23 February 2019, https://bit.ly/3nSg6O0. Accessed on 3 September 2021.
¹⁵²'Did Arnab Goswami Call Sachin Tendulkar Anti-National? Clip Goes Viral', *The Week,* 23 February 2019, https://bit.ly/3tLPbXP. Accessed on 3 September 2021.

Government policy in this context had been clear: not to play in bilateral tournaments in either of the countries. Past precedence was that we had played Pakistan on neutral ground in a multilateral tournament when military hostilities of a far more direct kind had been on. It was being pointed out that the stand taken by the Indian government in this regard, after 26/11 in Mumbai, has always been that India cannot host or travel to Pakistan for any bilateral series. However, the Pakistan team was allowed to come to India in 2016 to play the World T20. In fact, India had beaten Pakistan in the Asia Cup in 2018 in Dubai.

In such issues involving huge political ramifications, the BCCI has always been guided by government policy. I spoke to Rajyavardhan Singh Rathore, the then Sports minister. He was very forthcoming and cooperative. He reiterated the government position not to play against Pakistan in bilateral tournaments in each other's countries, but that we do play them in multilateral tournaments.

I tried to reason in my mind that wouldn't beating Pakistan again and again—in the league matches and in the knockouts if they made it—be a better tribute to our martyred soldiers? The economic consequences were nowhere in the CoA's scheme of things; we could afford to lose some money in order keep our pride and showcase our patriotism.

We certainly had a dilemma on our hands. The options, in my mind at least, were very clear, but there was a whole bunch of people with opinions who also had to be satisfied. This was the mindset with which we had a meeting of the CoA on 22 February. All the issues were hashed out in detail—all possible scenarios were considered. It was finally decided that since the stand of the government on terror attacks originating from Pakistan was to isolate it in all international forums, we should attempt the same. We needed to build opinion in the ICC to sever ties with countries from where terrorism originates. The

Indian representatives would flag security concerns for teams and officials during the tournament. It was also decided to seek the guidance of the government on the issue. There were, however, disparate opinions that the BCCI leaving it to the government was not adequate and it should have taken a decision to boycott the game.

In this meeting, the CoA also decided that they would not hold the customary opening ceremony for the IPL as a mark of respect to the martyrs. The amount budgeted for the opening ceremony—₹20 crore—would be made available to our martyrs' families.

In a telecast that evening, after announcing the BCCI's decision to cancel the opening ceremony, the anchor really took us to task and maintained that:

> The Cricket Czars of our country have refused to take a strong stand against Pakistan. After a marathon meeting which went on for hours, BCCI came out with a bland wishy-washy kind of response to the rising demand of boycotting Pakistan from all the ICC tournaments and World Cup and said that they have sought the guidance of the government whether India should play against Pakistan on 16 June in the UK.[153]

Fortunately, the panel lined up to discuss this aspect took the plea that politics should be kept away from sports and, in any case, this was a multilateral tournament.

Meanwhile, the CoA formally wrote to the Indian government seeking guidance on what course we needed to adopt. However, if past experience had taught us anything, it was that such letters do not evoke any response, and that is exactly what happened.

---

[153] Luthra, Chander Shekar. 'To Play Pakistan in ICC World Cup or Not, BCCI Puts Ball in Govt's Court', *DNA*, 21 February 2019, https://bit.ly/3fHh0bN. Accessed on 18 October 2021; 'India Upfront', Times Now, https://bit.ly/3tQ9Lq3. Accessed on 18 October 2021.

Sometime earlier, another reference to the government on playing a series with the PCB had not brought forth a reply either.

The reply notwithstanding, it is not for nothing that it is said that public memory is short. Time passed. February turned to March and on to April and May. Over these months, opinions voiced earlier were forgotten. Tempers cooled. Patriotism switched gears and was displayed on other issues. Come 16 June, India played Pakistan, and as anticipated, beat them. (India 336/5 vs Pakistan 212/6.) India won by 89 runs by the DLS method. That put paid to the entire saga.

BCCI VS PCB

Playing matches with our arch rivals invariably got the BCCI into unwelcome situations, and the responsibility of sorting out the avoidable mess landed on the CoA.

In 2014, when the BCCI was trying to push the Big Three formula for revenue devolution, and required a majority support in the ICC, it offered to play bilateral games with Pakistan in a bid to garner the PCB's support. PCB was, and continues to be, starved of funds, and playing India, whether in India, Pakistan or a neutral venue, is a money-spinner.

In the ICC Executive Board meeting held on 8 February in Singapore, resolutions around the Big Three formula were formally adopted by a majority. On 9 April, the PCB signed the letter confirming its acceptance of the resolution and addressed it to the then president of the ICC. On the same day, a letter signed by the then secretary of the BCCI, Sanjay Patel, was issued to the PCB with regards to a FTP on a bilateral basis between the two countries, in 2015–2023.[154] The last paragraph of the

---

[154] This was seen to constitute an MoU. It stated that the two neighbours were supposed to play six series in eight years between 2015 and 2023. Four

letter records that the letter was being issued in the context of resolutions which had been tabled at the ICC Executive Board meeting of 8 February relating to the new financial model and governance structure, and if, in June 2014, such resolutions were not passed at the ICC Annual Conference, then the letter would be of no effect. This was a heaven-sent opportunity for the PCB, who accepted the FTP offer and countersigned the 9 April letter. Soon thereafter, email exchanges between the PCB and the BCCI commenced to draw up itineraries for the bilateral games.[155]

On 26 June, the ICC had its annual meeting in Melbourne during which the resolutions supporting implementation of the Big Three formula were unanimously passed. Immediately after that meeting, the PCB started to press for operationalizing the MoU for bilateral matches. However, tensions on the border between the two countries were not conducive to the two teams playing in either country. A year passed with the PCB requesting for matches to be played. It was then felt the two could play at a neutral venue.

Usually, for India–Pakistan bilateral matches, the BCCI seeks a nod from the government. So, on 23 November 2015, Anurag Thakur, the then secretary of the BCCI, sent an email to the Indian foreign secretary mentioning that, as per the ICC FTP, India is supposed to play against Pakistan in a bilateral series either in the UAE or any other mutually agreed upon country in December 2015. Accordingly, Shashank Manohar, president, BCCI, had a meeting with Shahryar Khan, chairman, PCB, in Dubai. In the meeting, both of them agreed to play in Sri Lanka. The BCCI had therefore sought political clearance to play against

---

of those series were supposed to be hosted by Pakistan, 24 matches across three formats. The six tours would have constituted 56 games which included 14 Tests, 30 ODIs and 12 T20s.

[155]Farooq, Umar. 'PCB Says Six-Series Deal Signed with India', *ESPN cricinfo*, 14 May 2014, https://es.pn/3IuvAj4. Accessed on 24 January 2022.

Pakistan in Sri Lanka.[156]

No reply to this email was ever received.

Meanwhile, the controversial Big Three model was scrapped and was replaced by a model based on equity, common sense and simplicity, and passed in the ICC annual meeting in June 2017. The relations between the two countries continued to be strained and thus the bilateral series did not take off.

Not being able to persuade the BCCI to conform to the MoU, the PCB, on 3 May 2017, sent a notice of dispute to the BCCI under the terms of reference regarding the FTP of 2015–2023. Since by this time the CoA had taken over, and had to reply to the notice or remedy their grievance, we approached the government for permission to play with Pakistan. Once again, no reply was received. Certain parleys were held between the BCCI and the PCB officials, but no solution emerged.

On 29 November 2017, the PCB filed a notice of dispute before the ICC Disputes Resolution Committee, claiming:

i. The BCCI letter dated 9 April 2014 was a binding agreement.
ii. The BCCI had breached its contractual obligations to the PCB with respect to the scheduled November 2014 and/or December 2015 India tour of Pakistan. On that basis, the PCB, inter alia, claimed damages of $62,868,070 along with interest and cost.[157] The PCB's contention has been that the MoU signed by the erstwhile BCCI secretary, Sanjay Patel, in 2014, was binding.

---

[156]PTI. 'BCCI Seeks Government Clearance on Pakistan Series', Zee News, 25 November 2015, https://bit.ly/3fOXud6. Accessed on 21 January 2022.

[157]In the matter of proceedings before a Dispute Panel of the ICC Dispute Resolution Committee between: Pakistan Cricket Board ('PCB') and Board of Control for Cricket in India ('BCCI'), https://cutt.ly/JP5iIbs. Accessed on 18 February 2022.

Since the complaint had already been filed and arbitration proceedings were to be held in Dubai and contested under British laws, the CoA/BCCI had no option but to engage lawyers and prepare their defence. That brought forth further drama among the 'has-beens' in the BCCI. Considering that each 'has-been' was a self-styled cricket administrator and legal expert, too, the viewpoints that were aired in the media started with the usual—the CoA was inexperienced and that there was no need for them to attend the arbitration proceedings. This was from the 'guru' of Indian cricket administration. Each such 'pearl' increased our mirth in the CoA meetings. To quote a few:

> A former high-profile BCCI official, who didn't want to be quoted...attacked the Committee of Administrators for agreeing to 'fight' Pakistan, who will be represented by British law firm Clifford Chance. If the BCCI was run by a set of office-bearers who had the experience of handling board room issues at the ICC, India would not have faced this situation.[158]

How was one to tell him that it was the same set of 'office-bearers who had the experience of handling boardroom issues at the ICC' who had created not only this, but the whole trail of messy situations that the CoA/BCCI was finding itself in.

Our legal advisors, Cyril Amarchand Mangaldas, under the leadership of Indranil Deshmukh and with the assistance of Karina Kripalani, managed the entire briefing on behalf of the law firm engaged by us. They consulted with our counsel in Dubai and prepared all the case work. The list of witnesses was prepared. The then president and secretary were not available as witnesses. Finally,

---

[158] Bose, Soumitra. 'India Should Not Pay a Single Penny to Pakistan: Anurag Thakur', *Hindustan Times*, 30 September 2018, https://bit.ly/3FHaxrO. Accessed on 4 September 2021.

Sundar Raman, who was the then IPL COO, Ratnakar Shetty, Shashank Manohar and Sanjay Patel were listed as our witnesses. We managed to rope in Salman Khurshid, former External Affairs minister, to appear as a witness and give his perspective on how decisions regarding political clearance were taken in government. The hearing commenced in November 2018 and was scheduled to last for three days.

One of the primary defences raised by the BCCI was that it could not play the series with Pakistan in December 2015 because it had not received clearance for the same from the government, which was an essential requirement for the series to be held. Khurshid's presence lent credibility to the BCCI case. He made it clear to the panel that prior clearance of the Government of India in such bilateral cricket tournaments with Pakistan was mandatory and this was institutional SOP.[159]

After much nail-biting and pondering the catastrophic consequences if BCCI lost the arbitral proceedings, news finally came that the arbitration panel had dismissed the PCB's complaint. The ICC released a statement on their website, stating: 'Following a three-day hearing and having considered detailed oral and written submissions, the Dispute Panel has dismissed the PCB's claim against the BCCI.'[160] The website also carried a copy of the judgment saying that it was binding and non-appealable. The panel had taken into account the tense relations between the two countries and the various attacks perpetrated by Pakistan-based terrorist organizations in Jammu and Kashmir, Gurdaspur and Udhampur, in which several personnel had lost their lives. It had

---

[159] PTI. 'ICC Hearing: Khurshid Cross-Examined, BCCI Says Testimony Lends Weight to Its Case', *The Indian Express*, 2 October 2018, https://bit.ly/3nKvhbZ. Accessed on 3 September 2021.

[160] 'ICC dismisses Pakistan Cricket Board's Compensation Case against BCCI', *India Today*, 20 November 2018, https://bit.ly/3nJTf76. Accessed on 21 January 2022.

also taken note of the potential impact of these circumstances on the proposed tours.[161]

The Indian legal team, led by Indranil Deshmukh with support from Karina Kripalani, did an excellent job preparing for the arbitration. We not only won the case against the PCB but were also awarded compensation, which the PCB had to pay us towards expenses incurred. As is customary in arbitration cases, the BCCI claimed legal costs from the PCB. '…the ICC determin[ed] that the Pakistan Board had to pay 60% of the costs incurred by the BCCI—believed to be around $1.2 million. The PCB reportedly spent close to $1 million on the case.'[162] None of the earlier vocal cricket administrators welcomed the decision of the Disputes Resolution Committee, let alone congratulate the Indian legal team!

This entire episode stands out as a remarkable example of how administrators in the BCCI have put the institution's reputation and its finances to risk, merely to pursue their own personal agenda. This entire imbroglio into which the BCCI was pushed by the PCB had been started by the former in an attempt to push the Big Three formula through. Had the CoA taken the arbitration proceedings lightly and had our legal advisors not been professionally capable, the mess would have been hung around the necks of an 'inexperienced CoA'. But that has been the bane of the BCCI—its experienced and permanently ensconced honorary administrators.

---

[161] PTI. 'BCCI May Have Had Wish for Bilateral Cricket but PCB Had the Need: ICC Dispute Resolution Panel', *The Times of India*, 20 November 2018, https://bit.ly/3rE0j6l. Accessed on 4 September 2021.

[162] Lavalette, Tristang. 'Why the Pakistan Cricket Board Have to Pay Bitter Foe India $1.2 Million', *Forbes*, 24 December 2018, https://bit.ly/3qKpPry. Accessed on 4 September 2021.

PINK BALL ENCOUNTER

In the first week of November 2019, after the CoA had handed over to the newly elected body of the BCCI, I was happy to read a news item that India was going to play its first day/night Test match against Bangladesh. All credit is due to the then newly elected president, Sourav Ganguly. The fact that it was being hosted in his home turf of Kolkata, lent greater grace to the occasion. The Eden Gardens is a huge ground with a seating capacity of around 70,000 and was a befitting venue for the historic game.

Day/night Test matches had been proposed earlier for the Indian team to play but had somehow not materialized for a variety of reasons. However, on 22 November, I read another news item that quoted former cricketer, Mohinder Amarnath as saying: '...Baffling that Indian set-up resisted hosting day/night test matches...'[163] I have always respected the Amarnath family of cricketers: father Lala Amarnath, and his two sons, Mohinder and Surinder. I feel that Mohinder, like a lot of others, deserves to know why it took so long for day/night Test matches to be played in India.

To get perspective, we need to understand the history behind it all. In October 2012, the ICC recast the playing conditions for Test matches by permitting day/night Test matches. The first day/night game took place between Australia and New Zealand at the Oval in Adelaide on 27 November 2015. In India, in a meeting on 29 May 2016, the Technical Committee of the BCCI recommended that Duleep Trophy be played with a pink ball in the day/night format. A meeting of the working group held on 29 May accepted the recommendation of the Technical Committee and decided that Duleep Trophy matches will be

---

[163]'Baffling Indian Set-Up Resisted Hosting Day-Night Test Matches, Hats Off to Sourav Ganguly: Mohinder Amarnath', *India.com*, 22 November 2019, https://bit.ly/3tMrQW3. Accessed on 3 September 2021.

played with a pink ball and will be day/night matches.

It was further decided that based on the results of the Duleep Trophy matches, the BCCI would take a call on playing a day/night Test match using the pink ball in one of the matches in the series to be played at home in 2016–2017. Duleep Trophy matches were indeed played with a pink ball in day/night format. However, the BCCI has no record of any feedback obtained from any of the stakeholders of this event. Media feedback about the ball was: 'because of the brightness of the ball, the team handling the camera was able to track the pink ball better than the red'.[164]

On 27 September, the then BCCI president, Anurag Thakur, confirmed India would not play any day/night Test at home that season.

> It is too early to say anything [about pink ball]. As far as trying it in Duleep Trophy under lights is concerned, it was a big success. But you need to look at overall picture before you take the final call… I would like to go into details in a scientific manner to take the final call. As of now, we are not ready to implement pink ball this season.[165]

His statement put the speculation to rest, which was rife at the time, that India would host a day/night Test series at home comprising 13 Test matches. The season was expected to be played up to March 2017. So, that was for the season till March 2017.

The first time that the CoA heard of any proposal to play a pink ball Test was when Rahul Johri received a mail from James Sutherland, CEO, CA, on 11 January 2017, informing him of his intention to announce their home schedule against India for 2018–2019. Sutherland informed Johri that the Adelaide Test

---

[164] TNN. 'Pink Is Camera Friendly, but a Day-Night Test Far Away', *crickbuzz*, 31 August 2016, https://bit.ly/3tMs7Iz. Accessed on 3 September 2021.
[165] PTI. 'No Home Day-Night Test This Season – Thakur', *ESPN cricinfo*, 27 September 2016, https://es.pn/3KtpW2y. Accessed 3 September 2021.

match, probably the first Test, would be a day/night match. We need to take note of the fact that by then Australia had played four day/night Test matches. All were played at home, three in Adelaide and one in Brisbane. All four matches had been won by Australia—they had an unbeaten record in day/night matches. Their preferred venue for day/night Tests was obviously on home ground and that too at the Oval in Adelaide. Sutherland wanted them to play India on their favourite home ground (The Adelaide Oval) and that too in the first match itself.

Not to be taken in by this invitation, Johri replied to him on the same day that the BCCI understands that in a tour, matches are played in the sequence T20s, ODI and then Tests and sticking to the classic traditions of Test cricket—red ball/day matches. He reiterated that it would not be appropriate to make any announcement in this regard especially since the BCCI had not deliberated on the day/night format. He marked Gaurav Saxena AGM (Operations) and the acting secretary, Amitabh Choudhary in the email to keep them in the loop.

The next time the day/night Test was referenced was on 21 February 2018 when Choudhary sent an email to Johri, which Johri forwarded to the CoA. Choudhary had addressed a mail to the other two office-bearers, CEO and GM, Cricket Operations, enclosing an exchange of emails between him and the head coach, Ravi Shastri. He mentioned in the mail that the issue of playing day/night cricket had been discussed in detail with the national selectors, and CEO and GM of cricket operations. All seemed to be in sync that, under the circumstances, they would go ahead with the proposal of choosing one of the two West Indies Test matches for the first-ever day/night game on Indian soil.

This mail came as a complete surprise to me since no discussion on the subject had ever taken place with the CoA. We had been informed that the team was focused on the World Cup, which was to be played in the ODI format with a white ball and that the team was focused on that format. Other than that, it was playing Test matches as per the FTP in bilateral series with the usual red ball.

With that background, to have them change tack and begin to practise with a pink ball, too, merely to have the first-ever day/night Test in India, was definitely not a very prudent step. It was also rather surprising that the CoA was being merely informed that the management would go ahead and choose one of the two Tests to be played with West Indies in the day/night pink ball format. Now, I did not take kindly to this as even Diana had had no clue of such a policy decision being taken. So, on that day, in very definite terms, I asked this decision to be put on hold till all stakeholders involved had been formally consulted and a policy decision on when to play day/night Tests had been taken.

While the decision was put on hold, Choudhary informed the CoA on 6 March that he was trying to move forward in executing a policy decision which had been unanimously taken at the BCCI working group meeting on 24 June 2016. He claimed in that meeting that day/night matches with the pink ball had been introduced for the first time in the Duleep Trophy with the intent of using the said experience to have one of the home Tests in 2016–2017 season converted to a day/night Test match.

However, in stark contrast, speaking to the media after the said meeting, Anurag Thakur stated that the BCCI was in no hurry to play with the pink ball. The BCCI would wait for the players to decide on that and take a decision only when it was sure they wanted to go with the pink ball.[166] This was reiterated by him while speaking again on the subject on 27 September.

The CoA was never opposed to Team India playing a

---

[166] Gollapudi, Nagraj. 'Decision on Pink Ball Will Depend on Players' Feedback – Thakur', ESPN, 24 June 2016, https://bit.ly/3nJeBBA. Accessed on 4 September 2021.

day/night match on home ground. The issue was merely whether the team was ready to play in the midst of their preparations for the World Cup. In the next CoA meeting held on 12 April, we had a discussion with the head coach as well. He was clear that at that point of time, the team was not inclined to shift its focus to pink ball games. They could be ready for it after 12–18 months. I thought that should have been the final word as it is ultimately the team which is principally concerned, and the coach had made it abundantly clear that they did not want to shift their focus.

On a rather dull mid-week morning in April, while casually turning the pages of *The Indian Express*'s 25 April 2018 issue, I saw Choudhary's interview to Shamik Chakrabarty that quoted that, as far as the BCCI was concerned, there was very negligible opposition to day/night matches. On a specific question of whether the captain (Kohli) supported it, he answered that he had personally spoken to the head coach and that he was sure the coach, in turn, must have dealt with the team and sent in his recommendation. This caught my attention. Had we wronged the players? If they wanted to play and there was 'negligible opposition in the BCCI' why should we stand in the way? I hastened to consult my colleague and then requested GM (cricket operations) to get Shastri's specific views to make sure we were not on the wrong track. The reply from Shastri, received on 26 April, was not in favour of introducing the day/night pink ball format while the World Cup preparations were on.

At least in my mind the issue was settled till the World Cup.

On 30 April, another email was sent by Sutherland to Choudhary (with the CEO cc'd) adverting to some discussions that they seemed to have had in Kolkata, reiterating Cricket Australia's desire to have a day/night Test match in Adelaide. In the next CoA meeting held on 2 May, it was decided that the BCCI would not play day/night Test matches for the next

12–18 months. I have always felt that, going forward, day/night matches will be routine in every FTP, with the Indian team readily participating. However, without requisite practice with the pink ball, to go to Australia and play on their turf, that too in Adelaide, was not wise. It could lead to a rout and would demoralize the team tremendously. Choudhary was informed accordingly and was requested to convey this to Sutherland. The CoA was only being consistent with the decisions taken by popularly elected bodies of the BCCI.

This entire narration was only to set the record straight that the initial reluctance had been expressed by a team of elected and experienced office-bearers for the 2016–2017 season. The national team then got busy with the World Cup and at the first opportunity after that, the first day/night Test was played at Eden Gardens with Bangladesh. And that is why 'Kohli took only three seconds to decide to play a day/night test'.[167] It was a great event and I hope we will continue to play in that format. After that, in deference to the desire expressed by the CEO of Cricket Australia, we finally played a day/night match in Adelaide. We may have lost that Test, but we had to start sometime.

---

[167]Bose, Saibal. 'Virat Kohli Agreed To D/N Test in Three Seconds: Sourav Ganguly', *The Times of India,* 3 November 2019, https://bit.ly/3tKFhFW. Accessed on 4 September 2021.

10

THE NIGHTWATCHMAN RETIRES

A newspaper headline on the morning of 23 May 2018 read: 'Niranjan Shah's "Special" 70th Birthday Wishes for CoA Chief Vinod Rai.'[168]

The day comes every year; however, that year, it came with a special significance. I turned 70 on that day. It was only that the 'special significance' was not just for me but for lots of other BCCI/CoA/Supreme Court watchers, who were hoping to see the Court-mandated verdict of 'out at 70' apply to the court-appointed administrator, too.

Indeed, it was very kind of Shah, a very polite and affable person, whom I have met on numerous occasions. Since a busybody official in the BCCI 'on the condition of anonymity' had narrated to the journalist that Shah had sent the greetings by email, I checked my mailbox for the birthday wishes alluded to in the newspaper, but there was no mail from him. The postman didn't carry any greeting card from him, nor did the couriers deliver any birthday greeting. Shah had not called to wish me either. It seems that the busybody concerned had reportedly drafted the message for Shah but had not been able to persuade him to

---

[168]Gupta, Gaurav. 'Niranjan Shah's "Special" 70th Birthday Wishes for CoA Chief Vinod Rai', *The Times of India*, 23 May 2018, https://bit.ly/3tSDYou. Accessed on 5 September 2021.

mail it from Shah's email ID, even though it had promptly been released to the press.

Nonetheless, since I did not want to suffer the ignominy of being removed from the precincts of the BCCI headquarters, squealing and shrieking, as has been the fate of some, I thought I would verify if the age disqualification was applicable to court-appointed administrators. It is not always practical to keep approaching the Court for such mundane issues, so I contacted the court-appointed amicus curiae, the distinguished senior counsel, Gopal Subramanium. His reaction was that the upper age limit of 70 years was applicable to those seeking to stand for election to be an office-bearer in the BCCI. There was no question of it applying to court-appointed administrators. When I drew his attention to the news item and that it hinted that the administrators should 'walk the talk' since they were applying it to others, his retort was that court-appointed administrators could continue up to an age of 85 years and not attract any disqualification. He was very categorical. His parting comment was that all media activity was the wishful thinking of the 'dispossessed'.

That was that. I then decided that I better continue to address the issues that had been mandated to us by the Supreme Court. The most contentious among them was Uttarakhand and the Northeast being denied membership of the BCCI.

MEMBERSHIP DRIVE

Ranji Trophy is a domestic tournament in which all state teams are expected to participate. Each state is represented by a state cricket association, duly recognized by the BCCI, and that association is granted full membership of the BCCI. However, Uttarakhand, despite being granted statehood in 2000, was still being represented by the team from Uttar Pradesh. As per BCCI norms, only one of the many state associations which sponsor and support cricketing activity is allowed to become affiliated with the BCCI and have the right to sponsor a team from the state. The selection of the appropriate association is done by an elaborate procedure involving the inspection of all facilities and records of each association by an independent affiliation committee.

Representations had been made by different organizations within Uttarakhand to provide them affiliation with the BCCI. However, the laid down procedure had not been carried out for all these years.

This was quite a revelation. A mainstream state like Uttarakhand, despite having been in existence for 20 years, had not been able to field a team of its own. As a consequence, youngsters from the state were not getting an opportunity to play in tournaments, such as the Ranji Trophy. We recognized that this was most unfair to young cricketers of the state.

To remedy the situation, we sent an affiliation committee to assess the veracity of the claims made by various associations, to ascertain which was the best administered, had experience of conducting tournaments and had access to best infrastructure to represent the state. The affiliation team found that there were four cricket associations in the state seeking affiliation. Verifying their claims would take time and not permitting a team from the state till verification had taken its course would merely perpetuate this unfair treatment. Thus, as a first step, after rounds of discussion with the associations, it was unanimously decided to constitute a Consensus Committee of all the four associations so that they could explore the possibility of the state sponsoring a team for the 2018–2019 domestic season. This decision created a 'way forward' for the state to sponsor a team.

Over the next few months, after concerted efforts by a team of officials from the BCCI, led by Prof. Ratnakar Shetty and guided by Rahul Johri, introducing facilities for team selection and practice, organizing infrastructure facilities, enabling the use of a stadium and ensuring fair play in all processes were ensured. The Uttarakhand team participated and by the next year, one of the associations, the Cricket Association of Uttarakhand, was nominated as the affiliate association from the state. Similar were the stories of the Union Territories (UTs) of Puducherry and Chandigarh. Despite stiff opposition from various pressure groups, these UTs were also granted membership.

The Northeastern states had another saga to narrate. Sikkim, Mizoram, Manipur, Meghalaya, Nagaland, Arunachal Pradesh and Tripura had never been able to field teams in the domestic tournaments of the country as they had only been permitted associate/affiliate membership. The often-repeated argument within the BCCI was that they had neither teams of any quality nor any infrastructure. Obviously, no state was born with seasoned cricketers or cricketing infrastructure. It had to be created. The CoA called a meeting of the Northeastern states to try and understand their difficulties. Some had received amounts up to ₹50 lakh in 2009 but no further funds had been released. The quality of cricket that the state team could play notwithstanding, it was decided to start the process of enlisting these states as full members and have them participate in the domestic Ranji Trophy tournament in 2018–2019. BCCI officials, led by Saba Karim, provided all the support services to enable participation. The states were permitted to engage a limited number of guest players in the initial years to ensure that the standard of their team matched the other states.

Saba and his colleagues worked assiduously with the BCCI Technical Committee and charted different formats for the Ranji Trophy, the Duleep Trophy and the Deodhar Trophy. It was no mean job to organize 2,800 matches in a year, all over the country, for all the states to participate, in all formats. The challenges in terms of weather, ground, infrastructure and match officials were immense. They did a tremendous job, and for the first time, the effort proved to be a success with all the Northeastern states participating. Today, 38 teams representing 28 states and four out of the eight UTs play in the Ranji Trophy.

The next major exercise was to get the states to conform to the Lodha constitution. The mandate given to the CoA was straitjacketed. It did not permit the CoA any flexibility. The Court direction to the CoA was to implement the constitution as approved by the Court, first on 18 July 2016 and finally on 9 August 2018. It was only after P.S. Narasimha, the amicus curiae, was directed by the court order of 14 March 2019 to mediate on the pending interlocutory applications and make recommendations to the CoA/Court, that the Court afforded scope for some flexibility.

The first major area of disagreement was the 'one state, one vote' principle, which just about every member of the BCCI was opposed to. The CoA and the amicus curiae also favoured permitting the multiple associations in Gujarat and Maharashtra to be allowed to retain their membership for legacy reasons. The other issue was a number of office-bearers in the Apex Council of the state associations.

The BCCI Apex Council was to comprise nine members. However, the states had larger apex bodies and needed to have larger membership for various functional requirements. The state associations had constantly raised this issue. The rationale of their demand resonated with us, but we had no discretion in allowing it. Once the Court permitted the amicus to mediate and recommend to the Court, a practical via media emerged. This was an issue on which we jointly deliberated and on the recommendation of the amicus curiae/mediator, allowed the states to have Apex Councils of a size up to 19 members. This acted as a 'steam release valve' as states like Karnataka were permitted larger membership compared with states such as Manipur or Nagaland. I must compliment the patience of Narasimha, who heard every interlocutory applicant and recommended action as deemed appropriate to the Court. The discussions with the states itself took about 150 hours. For any senior counsel to take such pains was indeed very commendable. The credit squarely goes to Narasimha. This relaxation helped persuade many state associations to overcome their reluctance and fashion their constitutions around the BCCI constitution, as mandated by the Court in its judgment of 9 August 2018.

ALL-OUT WAR

This, however, led to some interesting episodes of how certain other states were brought on board. The readmittance of the Rajasthan Cricket Association (RCA) into the BCCI was another complicated issue. Its membership had been revoked in the BCCI SGM of 11 December 2017. The suspension was due to various internecine disputes between the RCA and its constituent units. The disputes were largely between the district units, such as Nagaur, which was controlled by Lalit Modi loyalists and the RCA. The SGM had imposed conditions that the suspension could be revoked only if the RCA gets the three districts to disassociate themselves from Modi and have them withdraw cases filed against the BCCI.[169]

Meanwhile, the CoA had to ensure that cricket continues unimpeded in Rajasthan by managing all the tournaments directly. So, though cricket did not suffer, the RCA was barred from attending the GB meeting of the BCCI, or be a voting member, till the suspension was revoked. The CoA negotiated with all the 'warring' groups, and on 6 September 2019, revoked the suspension.

---

[169] In the matter of Rajasthan Cricket Association's Suspension from membership of the BCCI, https://cutt.ly/QP5iFi4. Accessed on 21 February 2022.

It was then that the real drama commenced for the control of the RCA. The dispute was between two groups within the Congress party, seeking to have their man elected. T.S. Krishnamurthy, the former chief election commissioner, was appointed the electoral officer by an order issued by the joint secretary of the RCA (Lalit Modi faction). This appointment was not acceptable to the other faction led by C.P. Joshi, the president of the RCA and the then speaker of the Rajasthan Assembly. After much cajoling by me, both factions accepted the appointment. However, when Krishnamurthy came for the electoral role preparation process, the two factions clashed. The brouhaha became rather ugly and contentious. Krishnamurthy was distressed with their behaviour and decided to withdraw from the process. This became a challenge for us.

It was then that I felt the need to draw upon the experience of IAS officers who would have dealt with similar cases, multiple times in their careers. The mantle fell on R.R. Rashmi, an officer of the Manipur–Tripura cadre, who had just retired. When I called Rashmi, I found that he was in New York attending a conference. Nevertheless, not to be found wanting to accept an exciting challenge, Rashmi agreed to be the electoral officer for the RCA. He returned from New York, and the very next day took the flight to Jaipur. After assuming charge of the electoral officer, Rashmi threw the rule book at the different factions. He dug his heels in and took each faction/candidate head-on and, despite all the threats, ensured that the election was conducted properly. Had it not been for his firm and tactful handling of the situation, the RCA may not have been able to participate in the AGM of 23 October 2019, in which an elected body took over the BCCI.

Bihar was seeing its own pugnacious factions squabbling to take control of the BCA. There were allegations and counter allegations. The local media was full of the bickering that was going on. The CoA decided to constitute an independent supervisory body headed by Alok Kumar, a retired IPS officer who was the zonal manager of the anti-corruption unit of the BCCI. It was only after Alok and his team went to Patna and took over the entire premises and records of the BCA that some semblance of administration returned to the association. It was with Alok's firm intervention and his inimitable style of 'persuasion' that the BCA elections could be held and its nominee for participating in the BCCI election was also decided. Had Alok not managed the situation, Bihar would have been out of the election process.

PREPARING THE GROUND FOR ELECTIONS

On 9 August 2018, in the order approving the new BCCI constitution, the Supreme Court had ordered that the BCCI should register the constitution within four weeks and the states must register their respective constitutions within four weeks after that. The BCCI registered its constitution on 21 August 2018 and advised the states to follow the Court's directions and register theirs within four weeks. This started the second phase of filing interlocutory applications (IA), raising issues which had been discussed, debated and appealed ad nauseam in the Court. The basic issues of disagreement were the disqualifications on age, cooling-off period and being an officer-bearer in the state association for a cumulative period of nine years and the BCCI for another nine years.

It was to deal with these IAs that the Court had requested the amicus curiae, on 14 March 2019, to mediate and make recommendations to the CoA. While this process of consultation with the amicus curiae had commenced and attempts were being made to ensure that the states turn compliant, the CoA, in the meeting of 21 May 2019, announced the schedule for conducting elections in state associations. The process was to commence on 30 June and end on 23 September 2019. The BCCI elections were to be conducted on 22 October 2019.[170] It was also decided that we seek the advice of the Election Commission for nominating an electoral officer for the BCCI as his appointment would help the states expedite the process. On the suggestion of the Election Commission, N. Gopalaswami, a former chief election commissioner, was appointed as the electoral officer on 7 June 2019, and in consultation with him, the rules of procedure were prepared and issued.

Meanwhile, we continued to struggle with states such as Odisha, Goa, Uttarakhand, Rajasthan and Jammu and Kashmir to ensure that they could become a part of the electoral roll. So that state associations could expedite their election process, we finalized 23 September as the deadline for completion of the process. They would have to send their nomination to the electoral officer by then so that he can ascertain his eligibility for participating in the BCCI election. However, due to their own procedural issues, some states could schedule their elections only by 29 September and 1 October. In consultation with the electoral officer, we extended the date for the states to complete their

---

[170] BCCI Elections Schedule:
- **June 30:** appointment of electoral officer by the BCCI and preparation of the electoral protocol by the electoral officer of the BCCI in consultation with the CoA which shall be communicated to all the state associations.
- **July 1:** appointment of electoral officer by the state associations.
- **August 14:** completion of preparation of the list of members, election protocol and electoral roll of the state associations by the electoral officer of the state association.
- **September 14:** completion of state association election.
- **September 23:** sending of names of representatives of state associations to the BCCI.
- **September 30:** preparation of the electoral roll of nominees qualified for the BCCI elections.
- **October 22:** BCCI elections.

election process to 4 October to enable maximum participation.

Meanwhile, we continued to make efforts to enlist bulk of the state associations as compliant entities so that the election process could be completed, despite some associations furtively trying to delay the elections. The catch-22 situation was that they wanted the CoA out, yet not have an election. While these 'acrobatics' were going on, a bizarre situation arose, which created much mirth. The TNCA petitioned the Court to dissolve the CoA and form a committee of former BCCI presidents and office-bearers to supervise the administration of the game in the country. *The Times of India* interpreted this plea as: 'The former board officials are hoping to gain time and thereby scuttle the process by trying to weaken the CoA's position vis-à-vis the Supreme Court. None of the former presidents is eligible to be part of the aforementioned committee.'[171]

Meanwhile, after repeated and prolonged deliberations with the amicus, we found that more than 26 state associations had come on board and the only ones which did not seem to want to join were the TNCA, the Haryana Cricket Association (HCA) and the Maharashtra Cricket Association (MCA). This was their choice. Their absence did not matter to the system at all. In consultation with the amicus curiae, the CoA informed the electoral officer to continue the election process as per schedule.

While we were in the midst of all this, the Election Commission declared 21 October as polling day for assembly elections in Haryana and Maharashtra. Since holding our elections on 22 October would be cutting it fine, Lt Gen. Thodge proposed delaying the BCCI election by a day to 23 October, and I concurred with his proposal. This was done purely for logistical

---

[171] Indranil Basu and Solomon S. Kumar. 'Tamil Nadu Cricket Association Requests Supreme Court to Dissolve CoA', *The Times of India*, 12 September 2018, https://bit.ly/35fPsbr. Accessed on 5 September 2021.

reasons, to make it easier for people travelling from Haryana and parts of Maharashtra. However, as it was with other issues, the media misinterpreted the day's postponement as the CoA being divided.[172]

While the election did happen on 23 October, the electoral officer disqualified the TNCA, HCA and MCA from participating in the election. Despite being unable to participate in the AGM or election, representatives of those associations could not keep themselves from visiting the BCCI headquarters. They, however, had to be content waiting in the corridor while the AGM was taking place in the conference hall.

Towards the end of the CoA's tenure, when election to the BCCI was nearing and most of the states had conducted elections, there was widespread comment on how newly elected officials were proxies of the earlier office-bearers. An illustrative news item maintained:

> One of the objectives of the Justice Rajendra Mal Lodha Committee's game-changing reforms, which formed the basis of the Supreme Court's order 5 years ago, was to root out well-entrenched administrators. The administrators have officially called it a day, but unofficially, it is an entirely different ball game. The hold of the one-time strongmen is intact. Perhaps, even more firm.[173]

The article even quoted someone closely associated with the Justice Lodha Committee, 'We have done our bit, let the morality of it all and the violation of the spirit of the Justice Lodha Committee's

---

[172]IANS. 'Don't See Much Logic behind the One-Day Postponement of BCCI Elections: Diana Edulji', *Cricket Country*, 25 September 2019, https://bit.ly/32p79nT. Accessed on 5 September 2021.

[173]Sahi, Lokendra Pratap. 'Family Season in BCCI as Sons, Daughters & Brothers of Top Officials Take over State Bodies', *ThePrint*, 27 September 2019, https://bit.ly/3FVnka9. Accessed on 5 September 2021.

recommendations be addressed by Mr (Vinod) Rai.'

Indeed, a well-meaning and appropriate observation. The Lodha Committee has valiantly tried to block all loopholes. However, no committee can plug all loopholes to ensure that officials who have been 'dispossessed of their office-bearer statuses' should not have their appointees take over. Such a 'nicety' is expected of the officials themselves. However, why expect such niceties when even the FAQs listed by the Committee has been debunked by those seeking repeated electoral office, as 'figments of some lawyer's imagination' and not in conformity with the court verdict?

The reality is that state associations, as much as the BCCI administration, are structured in a democratic framework. The appointment of office-bearers is by a process of election, and elections involve mustering of votes. For election to the BCCI, the state associations do not take into consideration the competence of the nominated candidate; it is always the 'camp' nominating the candidate that matters. And let us not fault the BCCI alone. If a major state in the country can have its chief minister removed by a court order and then he nominates his wife to govern, with the rest of the country being a mute spectator, why expect the BCCI alone to display morality?

It is important to look at the issues objectively. It took the BCCI office-bearers and state administrators all of 38 months to accept the letter of the law laid down by the apex court. It is not that they willingly and happily accepted; they were taken to the water and just about forced to drink it too. This process took the CoA 33 months. In the very first AGM which was held within a week after the elected body took charge, the GB unanimously overturned the heart and lung of the Lodha constitution. They filed a request in the Court seeking changes in the 'cooling-off', and other rules pertaining to disqualification. No one has taken umbrage to this act. Then why blame the CoA?

The CoA's mandate was to implement the court verdict against a body of persons whom the Court itself had found 'intransigent and uncooperative'. Where was the scope for the CoA to look at the spirit of morality behind the reform process? 'Cronyism' is rampant in all walks of life. Dynasts have begun to control practically all systems where democracy is the underlying principle of selection. Why to have the BCCI carry a cross which is hardly considered a cross by the traditional standards of Indian democracy? Even looked at from the purely functional point of view, unless it is a 'family capture', if the proxies are managing the administration of cricket in an objective and principled fashion, why protest?

For instance, the Saurashtra Cricket Association has been at the receiving end of allegations of 'family capture', but it seems to have done cricket in the state of Gujarat a lot of good. On the other hand, the HCA, which has seen a family-run association in Haryana for many decades, with high-level representation in the BCCI, too, does not even have an international stadium to its credit where IPL matches can be played. Injecting morality into cricket administration, whether in the state or the BCCI, was never within the CoA's remit.

Considering that the CoA's remit was always being debated, the one question I was asked was this: which of my assignments—the comptroller and auditor general of India (CAG) or the chairman of the CoA—was more difficult? The two roles do not compare. The former is a constitutional appointment where one was in the top seat and could take decisions. There was a proficient departmental set-up which provided professional support under clearly documented guidelines. One took decisions and was accountable for the same. In the latter case, one was handed down a straitjacketed mandate and was required to implement it. The committee had no discretion. So even if one felt strongly about the impracticability of certain clauses, one did not have the discretion to digress. Neither job was difficult. It is just that the underlying conditions were vastly different. Both were interesting, what with numerous hecklers from the outside!

WHEN OLD ORDER CHANGETH

Finally, here is my take on the entire BCCI saga of 33 months. Kapil Dev, one of India's greatest cricketers, had led the team which won the World Cup in 1983. He soon moved on, passing the baton to the next generation. His contemporary, Sunil Gavaskar, proved to be a batsman and captain beyond compare. He too moved on. Sachin Tendulkar is considered God incarnate. He too announced his retirement from cricket. Both Rahul Dravid and later M.S. Dhoni are cricketers par excellence. Yet, why did they move on? Not only because their physical attainments were getting impaired; they moved on because there were cricketers who were younger, and possibly better, to whom they passed on the baton.

In January 2021, the Indian cricket team created history at the Gabba by winning the fourth Test against Australia and retaining the Border-Gavaskar trophy. Who were the stars in the game? None of the senior members such as Virat Kohli, R. Ashwin, Ravindra Jadeja, Hardik Pandya and K.L. Rahul could play due to various personal reasons or injuries. This caused no sweat to the young team members that included Washington Sundar, T. Natarajan, Mohammed Siraj, Shubman Gill, Rishabh Pant and Shardul Thakur. All these youngsters were playing their first series abroad. All they had was mere grit, commitment and application.

If the Indian team has such depth, do we have to keep falling back upon Kapil and Sachin only? So, if cricketers are made to move on, what makes our cricket administrators believe that heavens will fall on Indian cricket if they were to move on? The entire saga, which has created so much of adverse public opinion around the BCCI, from 2013 onwards, is merely because people did not respect the dictum of poet Alfred Lord Tennyson: 'The old order changeth yielding place to the new.'

EPILOGUE

Indian cricket is certainly in a very good space. We have a former successful Team India captain as the president of the BCCI. One of our greatest batting legends is the chief coach of Team India. Another batting legend is the head of the NCA. The team is led by one of our finest captains and the pink ball captain has led the most successful IPL team to a record number of victories. Team India comprises the best pace quartet of Mohammed Shami, Jasprit Bumrah and youngsters Mohammed Siraj and Shardul Thakur. The bench strength with the likes of Shubman Gill, Harshal Patel, Ravi Kumar and Avesh Khan is also very strong.

The women's team is in very good nick too. Veteran batter Mithali Raj continues to captain the Test and ODI team with Harmanpreet Kaur as the T20 captain. Smriti Mandhana and Jemimah Rodrigues are the batting strength whereas the likes of Jhulan Goswami, Poonam Yadav, Ekta Bisht and Deepti Sharma are the mainstay. These established cricketers have the likes of Shafali Verma, Taniya Bhatia and Radha Yadav as the Gen Next.

The tide for Indian cricket has certainly turned. While the post-Independence cricketing community comprised the Nawabs and the Maharajas, today's cricketers are children of autorickshaw drivers, vegetable sellers and coolies. There is the story of Shardul Thakur, who, I believe, travelled seven hours every day to attend cricket practice. Having come up the way they have, this is a fearless and courageous lot who will not take any nonsense from anyone, including cricket administrators. These cricketers are no longer at the mercy of the BCCI or any cricket administrator. They have the competence to make teams win and can make a difference to the side and hence can demand a 'market value' via the IPL auction. So, they are hardly at the mercy of their Ranji Trophy selector or state association president.

By and large, the objective behind the Lodha reforms is that cricket administration should be in the hands of former cricketers. They know the game well. They know where the shoe pinches and so whether it is the men's or the women's team, the players will be the central point of BCCI's planning process. Having a former distinguished cricketer in administration is also hugely instrumental in facilitating intra team management discussions. They speak the same language and understand each other better.

Hence, it was rather surprising to read of contradictory statements emerging from the team captain, board president, selectors and the like on the issue of captaincy concerning T20 or white ball. Why can we not sit down or use a phone and speak to sort out such matters? Why introduce the media as a medium of communication? What a dream run Indian Test cricket has had—the epic victory at the Gabba, and memorable wins at Lord's and the Oval. Virat Kohli has emerged as the world's fourth-most successful Test captain with 40 wins to his credit and may soon have emerged as the second or third behind Ricky Ponting (48) and Steve Waugh (41), who are legends in their own right. Does such a successful captain, or in fact any captain of a national side, not deserve more respectful treatment in splitting captaincy between him and any other team player over the white ball and red ball? Do administrators feel that we are legends of our own days and these youngsters do not need any other treatment than 'talking down' to them? This is where a former cricketer-turned-administrator must make a difference.

Kohli took everyone by surprise by announcing his intention

to step down from the team's Test captain post after the last match in South Africa. Kohli had made his debut as captain in the Adelaide Test when Dhoni announced his own stepping down in Australia in 2014. He has been a rare combination of leading the junior team to a World Cup victory and has been an eminently successful captain for the senior team. As the most ardent ambassador for red ball cricket, his emergence as captain brought an entire new culture for Team India. Fitness, competitive spirit and aggression were the motivating traits in Kohli's captaincy. In all these traits, he led from the front, hence, the dismay in public minds over his announcement of stepping down.

One very important feature of sound administration is marshalling the human resources of the organization. While team selection can definitely be left to selectors and the coach or captain, succession planning is a key characteristic that administrators need to address. Thus, even if the announcement of his retirement from Test cricket in 2014 had taken the nation by surprise, Dhoni had discussed the transition with the coach and selectors and ensured a seamless handover. So, while he was very much on the ground to mentor and guide the new captain, the new skipper was able to pick the strings of captaincy with ease and tact under his tutelage. It was an ideal relationship when the young captain gave all the respect and deference to the senior on the ground but, at the same time, the senior provided all the space and discretion to the captain to establish his brand of leadership. Each complementing the other, the duo made an unbeatable combination on the ground.

Every leader has his brand of leadership. If Dhoni was the epitome of calmness on the ground, Kohli was the picture of aggression and passion. This model was ideal for Indian cricket and needed to be adopted as a template. Thus, it did not speak well of Indian cricket management when the president and skipper were seen speaking at cross purposes nor did it toll happy tidings for team morale to see a spectacle play itself out in public domain.

A rather unusual step had been taken by the BCCI in appointing Dhoni as a mentor towards the end of the Indian tour of England. As having been the immediate past skipper under whose captaincy Kohli, Rohit Sharma, K.L. Rahul, etc., had played, maybe his presence in team management or in the dressing room could have been effectively used to either calm frayed nerves or provide a smooth segue from one captain to another, if the change in captaincy was imminent as per long-term succession planning.

It is for cricketing legends-turned-administrators to provide the succession plan to nurture the changeover and permit the incoming person to establish his brand of leadership to carry the baton forward. Let us hope we learn our lessons and take better care of our players, the skipper and team resources.

Appendix I

RESOLUTIONS ADOPTED BY THE GB OF THE BCCI (22 JUNE 2018)

Resolutions adopted by the GB of the BCCI at the special general meeting held at the Taj Mahal Hotel, 1, Mansingh Road, New Delhi at 10 a.m., on 22 June 2018:

Resolved that entire costs of this requisitioned General Body meeting for which 28 nominations were received will be borne by the BCCI. Resolved further to record with regret the fact [sic] that no officials were present nor that any official records available to assist the General Body as a result of directives issued. Agenda Item wise:

1. Consider and decide on matters relating to players' contracts and remunerations including remunerations to domestic players, match officials etc.
   'RESOLVED THAT the player contracts as tabled by the Acting Secretary for the season 2017–18 be and are hereby authorized to be executed for and on behalf of the BCCI by the Acting Secretary.'
   'FURTHER RESOLVED THAT the General Body principally agrees to enhance the remuneration of all domestic players, both men and women, and directs the Acting Secretary that all relevant information and

proposals be made available to the relevant committees, failing which, to the members of the General Body for their consideration.'

'FURTHER RESOLVED THAT the payment policy for players, umpires and match officials shall be revisited and formulated at the end of the 2017–18 cricketing season after considering the above.'

2. Update on and to consider and decide on matters pertaining to commercial rights and sponsorships of the BCCI.

'RESOLVED THAT the tendering of any commercial rights, sponsorships for and on behalf of the BCCI hereinafter shall only be undertaken by following the process as described which is part of policy and past practice.'

The policy and past practice referred to in the said resolution was described as under:

'There has been a transparent and democratic policy in place at the BCCI to deal with the commercial rights and sponsorships. The processes go through the administration and then the Marketing Committee and finally through the General Body.'

3. To consider and to take decisions on matters pertaining to the ICC including but not limited to revenues and the Members Participation Agreement.

'RESOLVED THAT MPA shall not be executed without the authorization of the General Body of the BCCI and the BCCI reserves all its rights regarding the Members Participation Agreement and regarding its participation in any other multi-nation tournament or games not covered by the Members Participation Agreement.'

'FURTHER RESOLVED THAT the Acting Secretary is directed to communicate this to the ICC.'

4. Update on and to consider and decide on the matter

relating to dispute raised by PCB in the ICC DRC. The members took note of the update.

5. To consider and to decide on matters pertaining to Committees and Sub-Committees of the BCCI, and other decisions of policy nature of the BCCI.

'RESOLVED THAT all committees constituted by the General Body from time to time which include standing committees, sub-committees, special committees and other committees constituted shall function normally subject to any specific direction of the Hon'ble Supreme Court in this regard that may be ordered by the Hon'ble Court.'

6. To consider and decide on matters pertaining to appointments and Human Resources of the BCCI.

'RESOLVED THAT the office bearers are directed to draft and propose a Human Resources policy for the BCCI and present the same to the General Body for its consideration and the proposal must necessarily include fair and transparent procedures and processes for employment, removal from service etc. as well as draft terms and conditions for employment as indicative guides for reference.'

'FURTHER RESOLVED THAT the house appreciates that the CoA may engage the services of professionals to aid them in their work of supervision of administration of the BCCI that they are mandated to carry out by the orders of the Hon'ble Supreme Court and such employments by them such as the COO(IPL), GM(Cricket Operations), COO(NCA) etc. are noted and it is directed that the relevant documents pertaining to the processes/ procedures adopted for their appointment be placed before the General Body for the necessary approvals by the BCCI.'

'FURTHER RESOLVED THAT upon the adoption of

the Human Resources policy by the General Body in a subsequent General Body Meeting, the process of filling up vacant positions and employment for and on behalf of the BCCI except those mentioned above shall be undertaken in accordance with the said policy in a transparent and fair manner and strictly according to the process laid down therein. It is made clear that all individuals who fulfill the eligibility criteria for each position as would be set by the Board would be eligible to apply for the given positions including those individuals who have been appointed by the Committee of Administrators.'

'FURTHER RESOLVED THAT till the appointment of the Head of the [Anti-Corruption Unit] ACU of the BCCI is done for and on behalf of the BCCI in terms of the above resolutions, Sh. Neeraj Kumar be and is hereby given an extension to his contract on the same terms and conditions as before.'

7. To consider and decide on legal matters and on the matter of legal representation of the BCCI in various forums generally and in specific matters.

'RESOLVED THAT in the present facts and circumstances the office bearers be and are hereby authorized to be represented before any Court including the Hon'ble Supreme Court by counsels of their choice in connection with their roles as office bearers that includes their rights and duties and other such issues that may arise in relation to the present facts and circumstances.'

'FURTHER RESOLVED THAT the office bearers be and hereby authorized to seek legal opinions, engage counsels, hold conferences in connection with their legal cases relating to discharge of their duties and responsibilities as office bearers of the Board and all such lawyer fees shall be borne by the Board.'

'FURTHER RESOLVED THAT the Board of Control for Cricket in India shall be represented in all legal matters only through the Honorary Acting Secretary of the Board.'

'FURTHER RESOLVED THAT the Honorary Acting Secretary be and is hereby authorised to engage counsels, appear, sign, verify, institute, declare, affirm, depose, make, present, submit and file all necessary notices, plaints, counter claims petitions, written statements, affidavits, undertakings, declarations, Appeals, Revisions, applications, statements, complaints, replies, responses, reapplication, rejoinder, vakalatnamas, power of attorney, papers and documents and all proceedings and matters in connection with any suit(s) or proceeding(s) filed by or against the Board of Control for Cricket in India before any court of law or any arbitration or any tribunal or any commission or any quasi-judicial or statutory or administrative authority at all stages and as may be considered necessary on behalf of the Board of Control for Cricket in India.'

'FURTHER RESOLVED THAT the Honorary Acting Secretary be and is hereby authorised to engage counsels, file and take back documents of opposite party, submit to arbitration and differences or disputes that may arise, in connection with or in may manner relating to the cases, or file, defend, prosecute criminal complaints before the courts of competent jurisdiction.'

'FURTHER RESOLVED THAT no other person including any employee of the Board is authorized or permitted to file any affidavits or to sign any vakalatnamas, engage counsels, appear, sign, verify, institute, declare, affirm, depose, file any plaint, petition, written statement, affidavits, undertakings, papers and documents and all proceedings and matters in connection with any suit(s) or proceeding(s) before any court of law or any arbitration or any tribunal or any commission for and on behalf of the Board of Control for Cricket in India.'

'FURTHER RESOLVED THAT the administration is directed to clear the bills of all lawyers and other such connected bills within twenty days of the verification of such bills by the Honorary Acting Secretary.'

'FURTHER RESOLVED THAT the Honorary Acting Secretary be and is hereby authorised to sign, submit and to give effect to this resolution and to forward a copy of the resolution to the relevant authority (ties).'

'FURTHER RESOLVED THAT this resolution supersedes any other resolution passed by the Board on this subject.'

8. To consider and to take decisions on all matters pertaining to the National Cricket Academy, its programs, and all matters pertaining to the proposed new National Cricket Academy Head Quarters.

'RESOLVED THAT all decisions required to be taken by the National Cricket Academy Board in accordance with the extant Rules and Regulations of the BCCI as detailed hereinabove shall be taken only by the National Cricket Academy Board subject to any order of the Hon'ble Supreme Court.'

'FURTHER RESOLVED THAT the National Cricket Academy Board is directed to examine and review the decisions taken in relation to the sphere of jurisdiction of the National Cricket Academy Board including but not limited to the processes and decisions of all appointments and conduct of programs etc. which have not been done following the correct procedure and due process and to present the same to the General Body with their comments.'

'FURTHER RESOLVED THAT the National Cricket Academy Board shall consult various stakeholders and devise programs making allowances for scientific progress in the field of sports sciences, future developments and growth and make recommendations for the requisite infrastructure for the new NCA facility to make it a state of the art facility.'

'FURTHER RESOLVED THAT the National Cricket Academy Board be and is hereby authorized to take all steps to develop and finalise plans for the new NCA facility at Bangalore and present the same to the General Body expeditiously to begin the work on the project in a time bound manner.'

9. To consider and to take decisions on all matters of cricket operations including those relating to the Domestic Season (2018–19.)

The decision taken by the General Body in the SGM is as under:

- All the teams presently playing Ranji Trophy shall play in the Elite Group of Ranji Trophy.
- The new teams, namely Bihar and the North Eastern States who are represented through the respective BCCI members shall play in the Plate Group of Ranji Trophy.
- The bottom two teams of the Elite Group (on the basis of points and NRR in case of equal points) and the top two teams of the Plate Group shall play a qualifying super-league.
- The top two teams of the super-league shall play in the Elite Group of Ranji Trophy in the following year and the bottom two shall play in the Plate Group of Ranji Trophy in the following year.
- This format would be applied for all age group matches as well. Both for ladies and for gentlemen.

10. To consider and to take decisions on the T20 Tournaments hosted and organized by State Associations.

'RESOLVED THAT the draft rules pertaining to the conduct of T20 tournaments by State Cricket Associations be and are hereby adopted with modifications.'

'FURTHER RESOLVED THAT a committee consisting of the office bearers and the Chairman, Technical Committee be and hereby is constituted to consider, report and propose to the General Body whether those players who have briefly appeared in the IPL may be permitted to participate in such tournaments subject to such terms and conditions that may be imposed.'

Appendix II

RAMACHANDRA GUHA'S LETTER OF RESIGNATION

Dear Vinod

It has been a privilege working with Diana, Vikram and you in the Supreme Court appointed Committee of Administrators. It has been an educative experience, spending long hours with three top-flight professionals from whom I have learned a lot in these past few months. However, it has seemed clear for some time now that my thoughts and views are adjacent to, and sometimes at odds with, the direction the Committee is taking as a whole. That is why I eventually decided to request the Supreme Court to relieve me of the responsibility, and submitted my letter of resignation to the Court on the morning of the 1st of June.

For the record, and in the interests of transparency, I am here listing the major points of divergence as I see it:

1. The question of conflict of interest, which had lain unaddressed ever since the Committee began its work, and which I have been repeatedly flagging since I joined. For instance, the BCCI has accorded preferential treatment to some national coaches, by giving them ten month contracts for national duty, thus allowing them to work as IPL coaches/mentors for the remaining two months.

This was done in an adhoc and arbitrary manner; the more famous the former player-turned-coach, the more likely was the BCCI to allow him to draft his own contract that left loopholes that he exploited to dodge the conflict of interest issue.

I have repeatedly pointed out that it is contrary to the spirit of the Lodha Committee for coaches or the support staff of the Indian senior or junior team, or for staff at the National Cricket Academy, to have contracts in the Indian Premier League. One cannot have dual loyalties of this kind and do proper justice to both. National duty must take precedence over club affiliation.

I had first raised this issue to my COA colleagues in an email of 7th February, and have raised it several times since. I had *urged that* coaches and support staff for national teams be paid an enhanced compensation, but that this conflict of interest be stopped. When, on the 11th of March, I was told that that there was a camp scheduled for young players at the National Cricket Academy but at least one national coach was likely to be away on IPL work and might not attend the camp, I wrote to you:

No person under contract with an India team, or with the NCA, should be allowed to moonlight for an IPL team too.

BCCI in its carelessness (or otherwise) might have drafted coaching/support staff contracts to allow this dual loyalty business, but while it might be narrowly legal as per existing contracts, it is unethical, and antithetical to team spirit, leading to much jealousy and heart-burn among the coaching staff as a whole. This practice is plainly wrong, as well as antithetical to the interests of Indian cricket.

I would like an explicit and early assurance from the BCCI management that such manifestly iniquitous loopholes in coaching/support staff contracts will be plugged forthwith. Yet no assurance was given, and no action was taken. The BCCI management and office-bearers have, in the absence of explicit directions from the COA, allowed the status quo to continue.

2. I have also repeatedly pointed to the anomaly whereby BCCI-contracted commentators simultaneously act as player agents. In a mail of 19th March to the COA I wrote:

Dear Colleagues,

Sunil Gavaskar is head of a company which represents Indian cricketers while commenting on those cricketers as part of the BCCI TV commentary panel. This is a clear conflict of interest. Either he must step down/withdraw himself from PMG completely or stop being a commentator for BCCI.

I think prompt and swift action on this matter is both just and necessary. COA's credibility and effectiveness hinges on our being able to take bold and correct decisions on such matters. The 'superstar' culture that afflicts the BCCI means that the more famous the player (former or present) the more leeway he is allowed in violating norms and procedures. (Dhoni was captain of the Indian team while holding a stake in a firm that represented some current India players.) This must stop – and only we can stop it.

Yet, despite my warnings, no action has been initiated in the several months that the Committee has been in operation.

As the mail quoted above noted, one reasons the conflict of interest issue has lingered unaddressed is that several of the game's superstars, past and present, have been guilty of it. The BCCI management is too much in awe of these superstars to question their violation of norms and procedures. For their part, BCCI office-bearers like to enjoy discretionary powers, so that the coaches or commentators they favour are indebted to them and do not ever question their own mistakes or malpractices. But surely a Supreme Court appointed body should not be intimidated by the past or present achievements of a cricketer, and instead seek to strive to be fair and just.

Conflict of interest is rampant in the State Associations as well. One famous former cricketer is contracted by media houses to comment on active players while serving as President of his State Association. Others have served as office-bearers in one Association and simultaneously as coaches or managers in another. The awarding of business contracts to friends and relatives by office-bearers is reported to be fairly widespread.

Had we been more proactive in stopping conflict of interest within the BCCI (as per Lodha Committee recommendations, endorsed by the Court), this would surely have had a ripple effect downwards, putting pressure on State Associations to clean up their act as well.

3. Unfortunately, this superstar syndrome has also distorted the system of Indian team contracts. As you will recall, I had pointed out that awarding MS Dhoni an 'A' contract when he had explicitly ruled himself out from all Test matches was indefensible on cricketing grounds, and sends absolutely the wrong message.

4. The way in which the contract of Anil Kumble, the current Head Coach of the senior team, has been handled. The Indian team's record this past season has been excellent; and even if the players garner the bulk of the credit, surely the Head Coach and his support staff also get some. In

a system based on justice and merit, the Head Coach's term would have been extended. Instead, Kumble was left hanging, and then told the post would be re-advertised afresh.

Clearly, the issue has been handled in an extremely insensitive and unprofessional manner by the BCCI CEO and the BCCI office-bearers, with the COA, by its silence and inaction, unfortunately being complicit in this regard. (Recall that the Court Order of 30 January had expressly mandated us to supervise the management of BCCI.) In case due process had to be followed since Kumble's original appointment was only for one year, why was this not done during April and May, when the IPL was on? If indeed the captain and the Head Coach were not getting along, why was this not attended to as soon as the Australia series was over in late March? Why was it left until the last minute, when a major international tournament was imminent, and when the uncertainty would undermine the morale and ability to focus of the coach, the captain and the team? And surely giving senior players the impression that they may have a veto power over the coach is another example of superstar culture gone berserk? Such a veto power is not permitted to any other top level professional team in any other sport in any other country. Already, in a dismaying departure from international norms, current Indian players enjoy a veto power on who can be the members of the commentary team. If it is to be coaches next, then perhaps the selectors and even office-bearers will follow?

5. Ever since the Supreme Court announced the formation of the COA, we have been inundated, individually and collectively, by hundreds of mails asking us to address various ills that afflict Indian cricket and its administration.

While many of these issues were trivial or clearly beyond our purview, there was one concern that we should have done far more to address. This concerns the callous treatment to domestic cricket and cricketers, namely, those who represent their state in the Ranji Trophy, the Mushtaq Ali Trophy, and other inter-state tournaments. The IPL may be Indian cricket's showpiece; but surely the enormous revenues it generates should be used to make our domestic players more financially secure? There are many more Indian cricketers who make their living via the Ranji Trophy than via IPL; besides, for us to have a consistently strong Test team (especially overseas) we need a robust inter-state competition and therefore must seek to compensate domestic players better. And yet, shockingly, Ranji match fees have remained at a very low level (a mere Rs 30,000 odd for each day of play); moreover, cheques for match fees sent by the BCCI are sometimes not passed on by the state associations to the players. We need to learn from best practices in other countries, where domestic players are awarded annual contracts like those in the national team, while their match fees are reasonably competitive too.

Several months ago, the experienced cricket administrator Amrit Mathur prepared an excellent note on the need for better and fairer treatment of domestic players. Both Diana and I have repeatedly urged action, but this has not happened.

6. I believe it was a mistake for the COA to have stayed silent and inactive when the Supreme Court judgment was being so flagrantly violated by people clearly disqualified to serve as office bearers of state and even BCCI run cricket bodies. These disqualified men were openly attending BCCI meetings, claiming to represent their

state association, and indeed played a leading role in the concerted (if fortunately in the end aborted) attempt to get the Indian team to boycott the Champions Trophy. All these illegalities were widely reported in the press; yet the COA did not bring them to the notice of the Court, and did not issue clear directions asking the offenders to desist either.

7. I believe that the lack of attention to these (and other such issues) is in part due to the absence of a senior and respected male cricketer on our Committee. Allow me to quote from a mail I wrote on 1 February 2017, before our first full meeting:

Dear fellow members,

I much look forward to meeting you all later today. I know Vikram already and greatly admire both Vinod and Diana for their remarkable work in their chosen fields, and am truly honoured to be working with them as well. I presume apart from discussing IPL, etc, with the BCCI representative we will get some time to discuss the way forward separately. I have several ideas which I wish to share with you about our collective responsibility, and wanted in this mail to flag what is most important of these. This is that we must incorporate into our committee of administrators, either as a full member or as a special invitee, a senior male cricketer with the distinction and integrity that Diana has. That will greatly enhance both our credibility and our ability to make informed decisions. The absence of a respected male cricketer in the COA has attracted a great deal of criticism already, much of it from important stakeholders in Indian cricket. It must be addressed and remedied. The amicus curae had suggested two outstanding names, Venkat and Bedi, both of whom were rejected because they are over seventy.

However, there are some cricketers of the right age and experience who fit the bill. Based on my knowledge of the subject, I would say Javagal Srinath would be an excellent choice. He is a world-class cricketer, was a successful and scandal-free Secretary of the Karnataka State Cricket Association and is an ICC match referee, and comes from an educated technical background to boot. I strongly urge the Chairman and the other members to consider approaching him in this regard. He would complement Diana perfectly, and the combination of these two respected and top class former cricketers would enhance our credibility and effectiveness enormously.

While Srinath is in my view the best choice, there are other alternative names too. I hope we can set aside some time at our meeting to discuss and resolve this issue.

With regards
Ram

P.S. Needless to say, I have not discussed this with Srinath or with anyone else.

I raised this issue in a formal meeting of the COA as well, but unfortunately my proposal to invite a senior male cricketer to join the committee was not acted upon. We should have approached the Court to take necessary action, or else incorporated a senior, respected, male cricketer as a special invitee. With such a person on board, the COA would have gained in experience, knowledge, understanding and, not least, credibility. Indeed, had we such a person on board, the BCCI management and the office-bearers would have been compelled to be far more proactive in implementing the Lodha Committee recommendations than they have been thus far. As the only cricketer on the COA, Diana's contributions have been invaluable; on many issues of administration and the rights of players she has brought a perspective based on a first-hand experience that the rest of us lacked. A male counterpart would have complemented and further enriched her contributions; but perhaps it is not too late to make amends.

    8. While all our meetings were held in a cordial atmosphere, between meetings perhaps there was not adequate consultation, and there were several crucial decisions made where all the COA members were not brought into the loop. For instance, a capable, non-political Senior Counsel representing the COA and the BCCI in the Supreme Court was abruptly replaced by another Senior Counsel who is a party politician. Surely other COA members should have been consulted by email or by phone before this important change was made.

I have taken too much of your time already, but permit me to make one last suggestion. This is that the place vacated by me on the Committee of Administrators be filled by a senior, respected, male cricketer with administrative experience.

Let me in conclusion thank you for your courtesy and civility these past few months, and wish you and the Committee all the best in your future endeavours.

With best wishes
Ramachandra Guha

Appendix III

EMAILS SENT BY OFFICE-BEARERS OF THE BCCI ON THE ISSUE OF ACTION TO BE INITIATED AGAINST HARDIK PANDYA AND K.L. RAHUL

(A)

From: Anirudh Chaudhry[174]

Sent: Thursday, January 10, 2019 12:33 PM

To: Diana Edulji

Cc: Vinod Rai; Amitabh Choudhary (Jt Secretary); C.K. Khanna; Rahul Johri; Karina Kripalani; Indranil Deshmukh

Subject: Re: Fw: Your interview on Koffee with Karan aired on 6 January 2019

Dear All,

I have not been asked to opine but this is a subject that I feel very strongly about and therefore I wish to express my views on the subject.

---

[174]Sharma, Jatin. 'BCCI Treasurer Anirudh Chaudhry Questions CoA over Permission for Pandya and Rahul to Appear on Talk Show', *Circle of Cricket*, 10 January 2019, https://bit.ly/3AbmB3t. Accessed 8 October 2021.

I agree with Mr. Rai that the comments are very crass and also that the apology appears insincere. I appreciate the step by Ms. Diana Edulji to seek the views of the legal team as it is absolutely essential that the correct procedure is followed in dealing with this situation since a faulty procedure would mean risking that the decision is vitiated ab-initio as was the case in the matter pertaining to the Madhavan Committee in the Match-Fixing matter in 2000 and in the matter pertaining to the 2013 IPL issue where the findings of a committee consisting of two former High Court Judges were held to be void and which culminated into the proceedings that led to the appointment of the Justice Mudgal Committee and subsequently the Justice Lodha Committee. Therefore, it is crucial that the correct process is followed.

Additionally, I wish to express the following points as they are of relevance:

a. Though I have not seen the Show Cause Notice, I presume it mentions the provisions under which the same has been sent.

b. The players who appeared on the show have definitely brought the game and Indian cricket and cricketers into disrepute by their words and admitted conduct. The consequences for bringing the game of cricket into disrepute are definitely something which will have to be considered. If I remember correctly, Mr. Warner and Mr Smith were banned for a year for bringing the game into disrepute and in conducting themselves in the manner that they did. While the ICC punished Mr. Smith for the offence of tampering with the condition of the ball with the maximum sanction available of a one Test ban, Cricket Australia banned him for a year. It would be pertinent to note that the Committee of Administrators had, in those facts and circumstances, also taken the decision to ban those players for the IPL 2018 and the Media Release dated 28th of March 2018 read as under:

'The Hon'ble Supreme Court of India appointed Committee of Administrators (CoA) on Wednesday took cognizance of the developments in the ball tampering incident involving Cricket Australia contracted cricketers – Mr Steve Smith, Mr David Warner and Mr Cameron Bancroft.

The CoA, in consultation with BCCI Acting President Mr CK Khanna, IPL Chairman Mr Rajeev Shukla and BCCI Acting Hon. Secretary Mr Amitabh Choudhary, has decided to ban Mr Smith and Mr Warner with immediate effect from participation in IPL 2018.

The BCCI hopes that the cricketers participating in the IPL hold the highest regard for the Spirit of Cricket and Code of Conduct for Players and Match Officials.'

Therefore, there is a precedence of the CoA having taken a decision in a case where the game had been brought into disrepute by players who were not even playing in the jurisdiction of the BCCI when the incident occurred.

c. I do not have the latest version of the BCCI contracts available with me and request that a copy of the same be provided to me. However, the provisions of the earlier contracts and the practice in place would have required these contracted players to seek permission to appear on the show. Was such a permission sought? Was such a permission granted? If so, by whom? It is very unfair that sports journalists who are essentially the people who bring the sport and the stories surrounding the sport to the fans and play a part in ensuring the popularity of the sport, do not get access to these players for interviews but Mr Karan Johar was able to get the access. I would like to clarify that I have nothing against Mr. Johar or anyone appearing on any show hosted by him or anyone else but I question the situation where the sports journalists are kept at bay while access to the players is given to entertainment shows.

d. Additionally, the intent of the Parliament in enacting the Act number 14 of 2013, The Sexual Harassment of Women at Workplace (Prevention, Prohibition and Redressal) Act, 2013 has to be kept in mind by us. The preamble to the said Act contains the following para:

> Whereas, sexual harassment results in violation of the fundamental rights of a woman to equality under Articles 14 and 15 of the Constitution of India and her right to life and to live with dignity under Article 21 of the Constitution and right to practice any profession or to carry on any occupation, trade or business which includes a right to a safe environment free from sexual harassment.

It is important to read these lines and let the import of this sink in, especially the reference to the fundamental rights of a woman to equality and her right to life and to live with dignity. It is in the backdrop of this that the comments made by these players on the show must be judged.

e. What also has to be kept in mind is whether the punishment, if the players are found guilty of violation of rules etc. or for bringing the game into disrepute, is going to be a token punishment or one that proves to be a deterrent for such acts and words. There can be no consideration whatsoever about the need of a particular player to bat at a particular position etc. when the punishment is being decided. No comparison with a former player is of any value or worth when deciding upon the quantum of punishment as that would only be giving validity to act in a derogatory, crass and disgusting manner if a player meets a certain level of talent and performance.

f. It must be noted that the comments such as the ones that have been made would definitely have painted a large, red target on the back of the players for potential recruiters for the organized syndicates who attempt to indulge in match – fixing across the globe. The very first caution that the ICC Anti-Corruption officers give in briefing to the players is to beware of situations of honey traps and the comments made on the show make it seem that the players may just be ripe for the plucking.

g. It must also be noted that these comments must have pained a lot of cricketers who have played for the country in the past with distinction and one can only imagine the pain they must be feeling that such comments have been made by people who occupy their former positions.

h. The Administrative Manager of the team must be directed to ensure that on the eve of the match and on match days, players are maintaining strict discipline regarding their timings and conducts as is expected of professional, contracted sportspersons.

i. Lastly, agents of players need to be regulated. It is a requirement of the Lodha reforms and it is a need of the hour if the stories that one hears from Australia are anything to go by.

As far as the quantum of the punishment is concerned if the players are found guilty as per the procedures laid down in the Rules and Regulations, keeping in view the above factors and discussions, a two-match suspension seems to be merely a stop-gap arrangement especially considering that the CoA had banned

Mr. Smith and Mr. Warner for a season. The players must be immediately suspended pending a proper inquiry and must be allowed to join the team (if selected) only once they have gone through a proper sensitization in addition to serving a ban, if imposed upon them. In any case the entire team and support staff must go through a sensitization process. The CEO may join them in the sensitization as well as recommended by Ms. Veena Gowda, Advocate.

In the end, I would like to strongly reiterate that the correct process must certainly be followed in dealing with the present situation.

Regards,
Anirudh Chaudhry
Honorary Treasurer
Board of Control for Cricket in India

(B)

From: Amitabh Choudhary[175]

Sent: Thursday, January 10, 2019 1:31 PM

To: Diana Edulji

Cc: Vinod Rai; C.K. Khanna; Anirudh Chaudhry; Rahul Johri; Karina Kripalani; Indranil Deshmukh

Dear Ma'am,

I have just seen this trail of emails. Had it not been for you Ma'am, the matter would never have reached the undersigned, which is yet another brazen violation of the BCCI constitution. Clearly, this was sought to be done consciously and deliberately, behind the backs of the office bearers for reasons best known to those doing it.

My response is as follows:

1. It is most unfortunate that the elected office bearers were kept in the dark about the course of action.
2. When a show cause indeed had to be issued, neither legally nor morally could it have been signed by a most tainted person himself. And I may add something as basic as this at least could have been understood by the person issuing instructions to the tainted issuing authority.
3. Suspension is in any case not punishment and for the reported misconduct, this suspension (pending inquiry) should have happened yesterday itself, consiering it was reported early (India Time). Therefore, the suspension must happen immediately.
4. It is surprising that the matter is being sought to be

---
[175]Ibid.

disposed of hurriedly and surreptitiously as in the earlier case of sexual harrasment.

5. Legally, the inquiry can be conducted only in accordance with the provisions of the registered constitution and not sought to be done by an 'independent committee'.
6. There is no way any society bound by rule of law will accept a verdict arrived at by a tainted person and the person who facilitated him to escape from the alleged grievous misconduct.
7. In view of the ODI in two days, the team/team management should prepare itself accordingly.

Thanks and regards,
Amitabh Choudhary

(C)

From: C.K. Khanna[176]

Sent: Thursday, January 10, 2019 3:56 PM

To: Anirudh Chaudhry

Cc: Vinod Rai; Karina Kripalani; DIANA EDULJI; Indranil Deshmukh; Amitabh Choudhary (Jt Secretary); Rahul Johri

Dear All

I have gone through the emails. As mentioned in the mails the comments by the said players are definitely crass & highly irresponsible. This is just not acceptable. We all condemn such behaviour. With such objectification of women, these players have a lot to explain. An apology is not enough.

    I suggest strict action & an immediate inquiry in accordance with the provisions of the constitution of BCCI. And an advisory must be sent to the BCCI contracted players & support staff.

Thanks & Regards
C.K. Khanna

---

[176]'Let Hardik Pandya and KL Rahul Play while Inquiry Is On: BCCI President Urges CoA', *The Free Press Journal*, 29 May 2019, https://bit.ly/33HyOAF. Accessed on 19 January 2022.

INDEX

#MeToo, 144, 145

All-India Senior Selection Meeting, 62
Amarnath, Mohinder, 103, 164
Amin, Hemang, 69, 77
annual general meeting (AGM), xii, 49, 84, 85, 166, 176, 180, 181
Apex Council, 14, 16, 17, 25, 101, 102, 103, 104, 105, 111, 148, 174
Arora, Sunil, 80, 81
Arothe, Tushar, 106, 125, 132
Article (19)(1)(c), 16
Asia Cup, 125, 126, 132, 156
Assam Cricket Association (ACA), 7

Bacher, Ali, 48
Balasubramanian, R., Justice, 5
Barnes, Sid, 67
Bedade, Atul, 138
betting, ix, 4, 7, 8, 11, 13, 17, 22, 87

Bhatia, Taniya, 128, 185
Bhattacharya, Trupti, 126
Big Three, x, 46, 47, 48, 49, 50, 51, 52, 54, 56, 63, 65, 73, 90, 158, 159, 160, 163
Bindra, I.S., 66
Bombay High Court, 5, 6, 7
Border-Gavaskar series, 72
Boycott, Geoffrey, Sir, 48, 63
Brabourne Stadium, 89, 152
Bradman, Don, 67

Central Information Commission, 30
Chahal, Yuzvendra, 72
Champions League Twenty20 (CLT20), 10
Champions Trophy, xiii, 58, 60, 61, 62, 63, 107, 108, 112, 122, 151, 203
Chandila, Ajit, 4
Chappell, Greg, 106, 124
Chaudhury, Anirudh, 53, 54
Chavan, Ankeet, 4
Chennai Super Kings (CSK), 4, 5, 10, 11, 12, 13, 38, 79, 82

Choudhary, Amitabh, 20, 55, 114, 121, 166, 206, 208, 212, 213, 214
Chouta, T. Jayaram, Justice, 5
Clarke, Michael, 70
clause 6.2.4, 8
Collins, Sam, x
compensation package, 31, 37, 109, 135
conflict of interest, ix, 5, 8, 9, 10, 11, 13, 30, 38, 39, 40, 41, 50, 59, 85, 103, 110, 111, 146, 197, 198, 199, 200
cooling-off period, 17
COVID-19, 86, 104
Cricket Advisory Committee (CAC), 40, 41, 102, 107, 112, 114, 115, 117, 118, 119, 120, 121, 122, 127, 137, 138, 139
Cricket Association of Bihar (CAB), 5, 7
Cricket Australia (CA), 11, 26, 46, 47, 49, 51, 52, 64, 165, 168, 169, 207, 208
Cricket South Africa, 51

Dalmiya, Jagmohan, ix, 46, 66
day/night match, 165, 166, 167, 168, 169
Deccan Chargers, 29
Deshmukh, Indranil, 161, 163, 206, 212, 214
Dev, Kapil, 90, 103, 104, 106, 137, 154, 183
Dhoni, M.S., 33, 34, 35, 183, 187, 188, 199, 200
Dravid, Rahul, 58, 72, 99, 112, 120, 121, 122, 183
Duleep Trophy, 164, 165, 167, 173
Dungarpur, Raj Singh, 88, 89, 90
Dutta, Nilay, 7

Edulji, Diana, 1, 38, 94, 103, 126, 131, 133, 137, 138, 140, 180, 206, 207, 212
Edwards, Wally, 49
Election Commission, 80, 81, 82, 178, 179
England and Wales Cricket Board (ECB), 26, 46, 47, 49, 52
expression of interest (EOI), 101

Fédération Internationale de Football Association (FIFA), 15
Full Members, 45, 47, 49, 50, 51, 52, 53, 66
Future Tours Programme (FTP), 33, 34, 35, 36, 46, 51, 52, 54, 65, 117, 158, 159, 160, 167, 169

Gaekwad, Aunshuman, 103, 137

Gambhir, Gautam, 90
Ganguly, Sourav, 40, 95, 101,
   106, 107, 114, 115, 116, 119,
   120, 121, 122, 124, 127, 134,
   149, 164, 169
Gauba, Rajiv, 80
Gavaskar, Sunil, 89, 104, 133,
   136, 155, 183, 199
Gayle, Chris, 71
General Body (GB), xiv, 14,
   25, 29, 36, 51, 107, 137, 150,
   175, 181, 189
Gibbs, Herschelle, 138
Gopalaswami, N., 178
Goswami, Arnab, 155
Gowda, Veena, 146, 147, 211
Grace, W.G., 67
Gray, Malcolm, 48
gross revenue share (GRS), 36
Guha, Ramachandra, 2, 94,
   109, 110, 144, 197, 205

Haryana Cricket Association
   (HCA), 179, 180, 182
Hayden, Matthew, 70
Hazare, Vijay, ix
Himachal Pradesh Cricket
   Association (HPCA), 92
Hotstar, 79

IMG Reliance, 153
India Cement, 5, 8, 9, 10, 99
Indian Cricketers' Association
   (ICA), 31, 102, 104, 105

Indian Premier League (IPL),
   2, 4, 5, 6, 8, 9, 10, 11, 12,
   13, 21, 22, 23, 28, 29, 33,
   38, 39, 40, 62, 63, 67, 68,
   69, 70, 71, 72, 73, 74, 75,
   77, 78, 79, 80, 81, 82, 83,
   84, 86, 87, 107, 109, 111,
   122, 127, 135, 142, 157, 162,
   182, 185, 186, 191, 196, 197,
   198, 201, 202, 203, 207, 208
interlocutory applications (IA),
   177
International Management
   Group (IMG), 68, 69
IPL Governing Council (IPL
   GC), 5, 10, 29, 62, 84
Isaac, Alan, 48

Jagdale, Sanjay, 5
Jain, D.K., 150
Jaitley, Arun, 80
Johnson, David, 138
Johri, Rahul, 26, 34, 77, 114,
   132, 144, 145, 146, 165, 172,
   206, 212, 214

Kaif, Mohammad, 90
Kala, Hemlata, 126, 139
Kalifulla, F.M.I., Justice, 10
Kamath, Nandan, 103
Kanitkar, Hrishikesh, 139
Karnataka High Court, 92
Karnataka Industrial Areas
   Development Board, 91

Karnataka State Cricket
  Association (KSCA), xiii, 91
Kartik, Murali, 90
Kaur, Harmanpreet, 126, 128,
  131, 132, 137, 141, 185
Khanna, C.K., 20, 149, 206,
  212, 214
Khan, Rashid, 73
Khan, Shahryar, 159
Khan, Zaheer, 90, 120
Khehar, Jagdish Singh (K.S.),
  Justice, 7
Khurshid, Salman, 162
Kimber, Jarrod, x
Kings XI Punjab, 82, 138
Kirsten, Gary, 138
Kishan, Ishan, ix
Kochi Tuskers Kerala, 28
Koffee with Karan, 148, 206
Kohli, Virat, 33, 34, 112, 118,
  119, 120, 137, 169, 183, 186
Kripalani, Karina, 161, 163,
  206, 212, 214
Krishnamurthy, Veda, 142
Kumar, Alok, 177
Kumar, Navika, 1
Kumble, Anil, xiii, 103, 107,
  108, 109, 111, 112, 113, 114,
  115, 116, 117, 118, 121, 124,
  137, 200, 201
Kundra, Raj, 4

Lalit Modi, 68, 175, 176
Lal, Madan, 139

Lamichhane, Sandeep, 73
Laxman, V.V.S, 40, 107
Limaye, Vikram, 2, 55, 110,
  144
Lloyd, Clive, 48
Lodha Committee, 12, 13, 15,
  16, 17, 24, 28, 74, 81, 85,
  102, 180, 181, 198, 200, 204,
  207
Lodha Panel, 13, 15, 17, 18,
  20, 109
Lodha, R.M., Chief Justice, 12
Lord Woolf, 44, 45

Maharashtra Cricket
  Association (MCA), 179, 180
Mandhana, Smriti, 128, 129,
  131, 141, 142, 185
Mani, Ehsan, 48
Mankad, Vinoo, ix
Manohar, Shashank, 46, 49, 52,
  159, 162
Marsh, Rodney, 88
Marylebone Cricket Club
  (MCC), 66
match-fixing, ix, 4, 22, 59, 87
M. Chinnaswamy stadium, 88
McMillan, Brian, 69
Meiyappan, Gurunath, 4, 5, 6,
  7, 8, 11, 12
Mishra, Amit, 72
Misra, Dipak, Justice, 1
Mohammad Ali, Qaiser, 38
Moody, Tom, 118

Mudgal Committee, xiv, 207
Mudgal committee report, 8
Mudgal, Mukul, Justice , xiv, 7, 45
Mumbai Indians (MI), 72, 82
Muralitharan, Muttiah, 69
Muthiah, A.C., 9, 90

Narasimha, P.S., xi, 174
Natarajan, T., 72, 73, 183
National Cricket Academy (NCA), xiii, 72, 83, 88, 89, 90, 91, 92, 93, 94, 95, 96, 97, 98, 99, 100, 101, 102, 109, 112, 185, 191, 195, 198
National Cricket Academy (NCA), xiii, 72

One Day International (ODI), 32, 81, 137, 166, 185, 213
one-state, one-vote, 14, 15, 17

Pakistan Cricket Board (PCB), 153, 158, 159, 160, 162, 163, 191
Pandya, Hardik, 148, 149, 183, 206
Pant, Rishabh, 72, 183
Patnaik, A.K., Justice, 7
Pawar, Sharad, 53, 65, 140
Pillai, G.K., 18, 103
Ponting, Ricky, 39, 70, 186
Powar, Ramesh, 106, 125, 127, 131, 138, 139

Prabhakar, Manoj, 138
Pro Kabaddi, 83
Public Interest Litigation (PIL), 5
Pulwama attack, 151
Punjab and Haryana High Court, 7, 45
Pybus, Richard, 118

Rahul, K.L., 148, 183, 188, 206
Rajasthan Cricket Association (RCA), 175, 176
Rajasthan Royals, 4, 10, 12
Raj, Mithali, 124, 125, 126, 130, 132, 133, 134, 137, 141, 185
Rajput, Lalchand, 118
Raman, Sundar, 8, 12, 162
Raman, W.V., 97, 138
Rangarajan, Shantha, 103
Rangnekar, Santosh, 35
Ranji Trophy, 15, 71, 72, 171, 172, 173, 174, 186, 195, 202
Rao, L. Nageswara, 7
Ratra, Ajay, 139
Rau, Purnima, 125
Rautray, Samanwaya, 3
Reddy, Bharat, 103
Reeve, Dermot, 69
Reliance Foundation, 82
Right to Information (RTI), 13, 17, 30
RISE Worldwide Ltd, 153

Rodrigues, Jemimah, 128, 185
Royal Challengers Bangalore (RCB), 82

Salve, N.K.P., ix, 66
Saurashtra Cricket Association, 74, 76, 182
Saxena, Gaurav, 34, 166
Scindia, Jyotiraditya, 36
Sehwag, Virender, 118
Shah, Niranjan, 54, 94, 98, 170
Shah, Sudha, 131, 140
Sharma, P.C., 146
Sharma, Rakesh, Justice, 146
Shastri, Ravi, 32, 34, 69, 107, 118, 121, 122, 148, 166
Shetty, Ratnakar, 32, 93, 162, 172
Shirke, Ajay, 5, 19, 55, 107
Shukla, Rajeev, 62, 208
Sibal, Kapil, 10
Simmons, Phil, 118
Singh, Barkha, 146
Singh, Hanumant, 88
Singh, Harbhajan, 70, 90, 154
Singh, Karishma, 1
Singh, R.P., 139
Singh, Yuvraj, 90
Sinha, Umesh, 82
Siraj, Mohammed, ix, 72, 73, 183, 185
Sony India, 79
Special General Meeting (SGM), 17, 18, 37, 51, 52, 54, 55, 56, 59, 61, 65, 84, 99, 100, 150, 175, 195
Special Leave Petition (SLP), 7
Special Purpose Committee (SPC), 7
Speed, Malcolm, 48
Sports Authority of India (SAI), 91
spot-fixing, x, 4, 7, 46
Sreesanth, S., 4
Sridhar, M.V., 32, 117
Srinivasan, N., 4, 8, 9, 46, 49, 62
Star India, 73, 79
state associations, xi, xii, xiii, xiv, 3, 14, 15, 18, 37, 58, 61, 72, 74, 77, 83, 93, 171, 174, 175, 177, 178, 179, 181, 202
Subramanium, Gopal, xi, 145, 171
Sundar, Washington, ix, 72, 183
Sunrisers Hyderabad (SRH), 79
Supreme Court, ix, xi, xii, xiii, xiv, xv, 1, 2, 3, 4, 7, 9, 12, 13, 14, 16, 17, 20, 21, 24, 28, 29, 30, 31, 40, 49, 58, 74, 75, 76, 78, 95, 97, 100, 105, 110, 127, 139, 145, 170, 171, 177, 179, 180, 191, 192, 194, 197, 200, 201, 202, 205, 208

Tamil Nadu Cricket
Association (TNCA), 52, 91,
179, 180
Team India, 30, 33, 36, 73, 90,
121, 185
Tendulkar, Sachin, xii, 40, 58,
70, 106, 107, 154, 155, 183
Tewatia, Rahul, 72
Thakur, Anurag, 19, 52, 159,
161, 165, 167
Thakur, T.S., Justice, 12
Thodge, Ravindra, Lt Gen.
(retd), 139
Times Now, 1, 157
Twenty 20 (T20), 9, 32, 67,
81, 82, 128, 131, 132, 133,
137, 142, 153, 156, 185, 186,
196

Ultimate Table Tennis, 83
Umrigar, P.R. (Polly), 88

Under-19 (U-19), 99, 113, 122
United Cricket Board of
South Africa, 48

Venkataraghavan, S., 88
Verma, Aditya, 5
Verma, Shafali, ix, 142, 185
Vishaka Guidelines, 145
Viswanath, G.R., 88

Wassan, Atul, 6
Whatmore, Dav, 113, 138
Woolf report, 45
Woolmer, Bob, 69
World Cup, 81, 113, 114, 119,
125, 128, 140, 149, 151, 152,
153, 154, 155, 157, 166, 168,
169, 183, 187

Yadav, Jayant, 72